A BOAT CALLED SCAMP

Dick Herman

Dick Herman
&
Friends

**Second Edition
2015**

A Boat Called Scamp

Small Craft Advisor
P.O. Box 1343
Port Townsend, Washington 98368
(360) 379-1930
www.smallcraftadvisor.com

Printed in the United States of America

Also by Richard Herman

The Peacemakers
Caly's Island
A Far Justice
The Last Phoenix
The Trojan Sea
Edge of Honor
Against All Enemies
Power Curve
Iron Gate
Dark Wing
Call to Duty
Firebreak
Force of Eagles
The Warbirds

In memoriam

Mike Monies
A builder and sailor

"There is nothing – absolutely nothing – half so much worth doing as simply messing about in boats."

Kenneth Grahame
The Wind in the Willows

ONE

Introduction

This is the biography of a boat called Scamp.

Normally, a biography is about a person, or, at least, a living thing, like the small and ungainly Seabiscuit, the famous Thoroughbred who surprised the world. Scamp, like Seabiscuit, is small and looks a bit ungainly, but with both, the image belies the soul beneath.

Some may question the analogy. How can a small, awkward looking boat with a snub nose and odd-looking sail be compared to a horse with the heart of a champion? Sailboats don't have hearts or personalities, much less souls. However, there is a breed of sailor out there who would disagree. Small craft sailors know, with certainty in their hearts, that boats can and do have personalities. For many of them, including the author of this biography, Scamp is the proof.

Officially, its name is SCAMP, for Small Craft Advisor Magazine Project. However, this narrative uses the traditional form, Scamp, as the frequent use of the acronym in capital letters is distracting. Webster's Dictionary lists the primary definition of "scamp" as "rascal" and the secondary meaning as "an impish or playful young person." Scamp is not a mean, difficult, or deceptive boat in any sense, and it is a remarkably stable and playful craft. Considering what it is, and the role of the editors of *Small Craft Advisor* magazine in its creation, it is well named.

The Scamp started in the dreams of a teenager over twenty-five years ago, and came into being because of a fortuitous confluence of a number of individuals. Each left his mark on the boat as it progressed from imagination, through conception, to the drawing board, to the initial construction, and finally to the reality of sailing. They are not the main players on the world's stage, although one is leaving an indelible mark on the environment. Yet, it is an impressive cast of characters and each has certain uncommon traits and skills. It is because they touched Scamp in their own way that Scamp is what it is, taking a little from each.

Not all small craft sailors are given to deep philosophical or introspective thought. Many would rather be on the water, sailing their boats. Yet, in quiet moments, perhaps over a glass of wine at dockside, or on the beach and in the company of friends, they will share a reflective thought.

There is nothing earthshaking in their insights, but listen carefully and you can hear themes as old as the written word. There is always the challenge of making safe harbor, and the adage "The smaller the boat, the bigger the adventure" holds true. There is a deep respect for honesty of design and a love of sweeping lines that satisfies an indefinable need. It is simply there, perhaps in our genetic makeup. As a consequence, we ask the reader's indulgence if we never answer the basic question "Why Scamp?" But like sailing Scamp, it will be fun searching for clues.

In a very real sense, this narrative is about the individuals who helped give birth to that teenager's dream. But in the end, this story is about a small craft that sails with a perky confidence and a personality all its own, announcing to the world "Here I am!"

TWO

Beginnings

Launchings

It was a perfect day for a sail as the small crowd gathered in the courtyard of the Northwest Maritime Center in Port Townsend, Washington. The weather was sunny with a light breeze, and the temperature hovered in the fifties—that's Fahrenheit, not Celsius. They stood quietly as the big doors to the workshop opened and Joshua Colvin, with the help of a few friends, carried a small sailboat out and set it on a temporary trailer. The crowd made all the requisite comments that befitted the first appearance of a new design, and the name "Scamp" was heard over and over as they took the boat's measure.

A few noted the time and day. It was three o'clock in the afternoon, Wednesday, November 10, 2010, when Scamp made its debut.

Many were beguiled by the appearance of the new boat—quite an achievement as the Port Townsend area is a Mecca for traditional wooden boats on the West Coast. At first glance,

Scamp's traditional-looking hull with its pram bow and single sail gives no indication of what lies beneath, for it is a small sailboat —eleven-foot eleven-inches long—and for many casual observers, their first reaction when seeing it setting on its trailer is "What a cute little boat!" They will meander past, pause and turn around. Then something unusual happens. They walk back, stand close, and touch it, often stroking it like a pet. Many shake their heads and mutter something about Scamp being homely or ugly, and if they stand there long enough, start to smile. Scamp affects people that way and no one is really sure why.

With more than a little help from his friends, Josh pushed the little craft over to the launch ramp on the far side of the Maritime Center. Josh said the traditional words that go with the launching of a newly created boat. He gave a warm-hearted thanks to the designer, John Welsford, along with the three skilled artisans, Kees Prins, Scott Jones, and Sarah Rudolph, who actually built the craft. He mentioned Brandon Davis at Turn Point Design, and Simeon Baldwin. Even today, mention Scamp to any of them and you will be left with the distinct impression you are talking to proud parents. Josh popped open a bottle of champagne and offered the traditional toast.

It was time.

They rolled Scamp into the water. It was an exciting moment for Josh as the boat floated free; would she float on her lines? Would she capsize? It has been known to happen. Josh held onto the painter as Scamp immediately found a balanced trim. She sat high in the water with no ballast, gear or crew aboard and Josh breathed easier. He was not alone. His wife, Anika, had been watching with pride for she knew the time and effort

Josh had invested in the boat. However, there was no doubt she was holding her breath as Scamp floated free, and she wouldn't relax until the boat sailed safely away.

Scamp pulled at her painter, eager to get underway as Josh and Simeon climbed aboard. The winds were still very light so the two men did not pull the plug on the internal water ballast tank and take on the 175 pounds. Gaining confidence by the minute, they hoisted the sail, not bothering to set a reef, and gave a few strokes on the oars to bring Scamp about. That was their first surprise. Even with two men on board, Scamp rowed easily. They set the sail and were off. As expected, the lug rig was easy to control and tune, and it seemed to point well, although they didn't try for any measurements. They fiddled with the downhaul and cleared any wrinkles in the sail.

Designers and boat builders like to talk about "ergonomics," probably because it addresses so many issues. But for the average skipper, it only means one thing: is the boat comfortable? Again, there were no surprises as John Welsford had designed Scamp with a roomy cockpit where everything fell easily to hand. The seating was comfortable and two crew don't knock knees as they move about, as they might even on many larger boats.

Part of the charm of Scamp is its "veranda," an open cuddy cabin that is neither a cuddy nor a cabin but more like a hard dodger. It is the perfect place to take refuge from the elements, out of the wind or rain, but still remain part of the action. Josh had a chance to experience that as the sun neared the western horizon and the temperature cooled.

It was time to head for the dock. The light air was right off the beach, and Scamp had no trouble sailing back. On shore, the most heard comment was how she looked like a much bigger boat out there. Willing hands helped pull the boat out and get it back on its trailer as the weather cooled. Josh and Simeon had learned a lot from that first sail and trusted the boat. But they needed a real test day to shake the boat out and discover what it was truly made of. They didn't have to wait long.

Photo: Debra Colvin
First Sail
Josh Colvin and Simeon Baldwin launch Scamp

The next morning, Josh looked out the window. The weather was overcast and the winds a constant twenty-five knots and gusting. The phone rang. It was Kees Prins, the lead builder for Scamp at the Northwest Maritime Center. Josh could hear the wind whistling in the background, and he asked Kees a simple question, "You ready?"

"Let's go."

The date was November 11, 2010, and the number still rings in Josh's ear. Scamp is exactly eleven-feet eleven-inches long, matching the date of 11/11. Any gambler knows the significance of eleven when shooting craps, and there is a small Seven-Eleven convenience store almost everywhere, ready to help folks get through the day. The date 9-11 carries an emotional impact for Americans, and on the eleventh hour, of the eleventh day, of the eleventh month of 1918, the guns fell silent in northern France, ending World War I. And on the eleventh day of the eleventh month, in the year 2010, Scamp was truly put to its first test, a daunting task for a craft not even two days old.

Josh and Kees met fifteen minutes later, and quickly dropped the boat back into the water. This time there was no question—the water ballast tank would be filled. Kees suggested they set a single reef. "How about two?" Josh said. They climbed aboard and sailed around the marina for a few minutes, seeing how she would respond in the higher winds. A balanced lug has a "best" side, and a "compromised" side where the wind pushes the forward part of the sail against the mast. They were delighted to discover that it made little difference as to the tack.

The 175-pound water ballast helped immensely, and Josh laughingly recalls the dinghy feeling like an icebreaker. Small craft sailors are like that, jumping to big conclusions about small things. (See above comments about the number eleven.) Outside the marina, whitecaps and big swells were beckoning, which was why they were there.

They raced out the entrance of the marina, and into the environment John Welsford had envisioned for Scamp. Kees was at the helm and Josh was waiting for a scary jibe, or for the boat to fail coming through a tack, or for some other glitch to raise its troublesome head—small stuff like the centerboard breaking free or the rudder falling off. None of that happened, even though the conditions gave real meaning to the word "sporting." Within a few minutes, they were relaxed and zipping all over the place, the only sailboat on the water.

The small craft was in its element, and Kees bellowed "Scamp!" at the top of his lungs.

Later that day, Josh sent John Welsford an "ahoy" via e-mail, recounting the first two launches. He ended with a simple, "Thanks again for your great work." It was a classic understatement the New Zealander appreciated.

Scamp had passed its first test.

Lineages

Like most things, sailboats have a lineage and Scamp is no exception. The origins of some boats are lost, and it falls to the historians to speculate about the genesis of craft such as the Irish curragh, which can trace its lineage to ancient Mesopotamia over 5000 years ago. Others, like the graceful clipper ships of the 19th Century, can be attributed to the Baltimore clippers developed in the Chesapeake Bay in the 18th Century. The names of designers and builders like Donald McKay came to be attached to the beautiful ships, which are considered the epitome of The Age of Sail.

With the Age of Power, sailboats transitioned into mostly pleasure and racing craft, but even today, lateen-rigged falluccas ply the waters of the Middle East, fishing, and carrying cargo and unsuspecting tourists beguiled by their exotic appearance. Designers like Nathanael Herreshoff were soon associated with the ongoing America's Cup rivalry. Later, individuals like Drake Sparkman and Olin Stephens became known for the design and production of famous, big, and expensive, yachts.

That world still exists, but sailing behind the glamorous media darlings are a huge number of small, relatively inexpensive sailboats with their own histories and following. Designers like Phil Bolger, Graham Byrnes, Gary Dierking, Dudley Dix, Paul Fisher, Ross Lillistone, Jim Michalak, Michael Storer, Francois Vivier, and Richard Woods have delighted small craft sailors with their creations for years. One of the foremost is John Welsford, a self-taught designer from New Zealand, who gave life to Scamp.

But the idea didn't start with John Welsford, or in New Zealand. Scamp's story is so firmly linked to Joshua Colvin and Craig Wagner, the publishers of *Small Craft Advisor* magazine, that to understand Scamp calls for a brief look at the two men, their magazine, and Port Townsend, for that is the context of Scamp.

Joshua stands just shy of six feet tall, is trim and fit, and his brown hair, hazel eyes, and youthful appearance belies a man in his early forties. He was born in Los Angeles, California, in 1971 during the Sylmar Earthquake that registered 6.6 on the Richter scale, which, for anyone who has experienced a 6.6, is a whole lot of shaking going on. The exact significance of this on his later career is unknown. After that, his parents moved often, following their careers. Josh gave college a shot, first at San Diego State, and then Sacramento Community College before becoming a fashion photographer. Later, in South Miami Beach, Florida, he started a clothing company with a friend. "Hooligan" featured an urban line of clothes that spread to seventeen countries before he moved on to owning two retail surf shops in the San Luis Obispo California area.

It was there, while exchanging ideas with his uncle and best friend, Craig Wagner, that the idea of a magazine was born. Making the commitment to start a magazine requires a huge leap of faith, and job security is not part of the equation, but the two men gave it a go, bringing out their first issue of *Small Craft Advisor* in January 2000. Coincidentally, that was the year Josh and Anika were married.

Craig Wagner is a personable and intensely private individual. His dad and uncle were very water oriented—body surfers and the like—as they lived near the beach in New Jersey. Later, both served in the Navy during WW II, and, as a result, water and boats have always been part of Craig's life. He fondly remembers spending hours lost in a thick old copy of the Bluejacket's Manual in the late 1940s.

As a young teen in Los Angeles, he and a good buddy spent many a summer morning drifting down the Balona Creek storm drain on truck inner tubes, reaching the ocean at Playa del Rey. Resourceful water rats, they would rig broomstick masts with bed-sheet sails and catch the afternoon onshore breeze for the drift home. "When I became a bit more sophisticated, I'd hitchhike to the old lagoon where Marina del Rey is today, and spend afternoons crisscrossing the water in a rented 50-cent-an-hour sailing dinghy, all the while daydreaming of boats I'd eventually own, and the faraway places they'd take me."

It was in 1999 when Craig and Josh decided they wanted a sailboat, and they teamed up building a Glen-L Minuet. The Minuet is a salty-looking fifteen-foot sloop with a cabin and bowsprit, which appealed to the two partners. Displacing over eleven hundred-pounds with a centerboard makes it more than a sailing dinghy, and, consequently, more challenging to build.

Craig recalls, "We soon felt things weren't moving quickly enough, so we decided we'd each buy a used small sailboat. This got us searching magazines for performance comparisons." That was when the reality of sailing magazines kicked in—very little information was available that really spelled out which boats did what best. Craig is not sure why, but speculates that "Perhaps magazines at the time were afraid candor might cost them boat-manufacturer ad revenue."

Anyone who sails small craft knows they can capsize and things can go wrong at an alarming rate; it is part of the challenge, and charm, of sailing them. It is for good reason that Josh and Craig's magazine carries the subtitle of "Small Boats – Big Adventure." Later on, they would experience exactly what magazine publishers are up against.

Their pot was boiling with building the Minuet, researching small craft to purchase, and thoughts of starting a magazine when they began thinking of organizing a race to finally determine the "unvarnished truth" as to which boats did what best. It was about this time they made the acquaintance of Judy Blumhorst, the then commodore of the Potter Yachters of Northern California.

Commodore Judy is a trim, supercharged sailing enthusiast who owns a small fleet of small craft, including *Little Deuce Sloop*, a highly modified West Wight Potter 19 that is amazingly fast. She and Jerry Barrilleaux, who sails *Sunshine*, a stock West Wight Potter 18, with skill, cunning and speed, had been in a friendly dispute with Montgomery skippers as to which boat was the fastest microcruiser. The idea of a race, or more specifically a "friendly" challenge between microcruisers actually configured for cruising and not racing, was in the formative stages. As sailing clubs go, the Potter Yachters is a large and very active organization, and the membership supported the idea.

It was in the Oakland California estuary when the Potter Yachter Cruiser Challenge, sponsored by *Small Craft Advisor*, became a reality in the summer of 1999. It was an instant hit with the small-sailboat crowd. Now Josh and Craig had something to write about. The first issue of *Small Craft Advisor* reported the race results, along with an interesting interview with small-boat adventurer David Omick, and a review of the Com-Pac 19. Within a few issues, the small 6.5 x 10 inch, black and white printed journal with its plain brown cover was a staple in the small craft community.

Early on, Josh and Craig had to make a critical decision. They knew all too well what the inherent limitations of small craft were. They capsize, they have limited range, and they are much more subject to the elements than their larger brothers and sisters. A small-craft skipper is much more involved in actual sailing rather than managing the craft's systems. It's like the difference between flying a Piper Cub and a Boeing 747.

But experience pays dividends when the chips are down. Just ask the skipper of a bluewater racer who he or she wants at the helm in a storm—the person who raced dinghies. Were Josh and Craig going to defend the advertisers or look out for their readers? As Josh carefully explains, "Ultimately, it is always about the reader." Then he adds, "That's also why don't discuss politics, religion, or raising children." To date, they have held true to that policy and let the chips fall where they may. It has proven to be a good policy, and they are very proud of sailing and reviewing nearly a hundred boats.

They are also proud of their "Seaworthiness & Trailerable Sailboat" test first published in the Sep/Oct 2007 (issue #47), of *Small Craft Advisor*. They enlisted the help of John Vigor, the author of "The Seaworthy Offshore Sailboat," and eleven other books devoted to sailing and boating reference. As he has sailed eleven-foot Mirror-class dinghies for thirty years and sailed more than 15,000 ocean miles in boats 11 to 40 feet, his credentials are impeccable. Together, they set the criteria for the type of boat they were evaluating, and John stated it simply and succinctly in that issue.

The following quiz will give you an indication of the seaworthiness of your trailerable sailboat of not more than 3,500 pounds displacement, used in areas and weather conditions for which it was designed. In general, that means the conditions found in the protected and semi-protected waters typically frequented by trailer sailors . . . . Incidentally, don't jump off a cliff if your boat doesn't come up to your expectations. There are certain seaworthy designs that fall through the cracks in our quiz. . . . What we hope is that taking the quiz will make you think more deeply about the many factors that constitute seaworthiness in a small sailboat . . . . Finally, we hope a good score will bring you improved confidence in your choice of boat and greater pleasure in sailing her.

(The test is available online at www.smallcraftadvisor.com. The skipper of any small craft who is thinking of poking his bow into the open ocean should consider taking it.)

Since its inception, the magazine has undergone a metamorphosis, transitioning from a small format with a simple brown cover, to a regular-sized glossy magazine with a color cover. With the fall 2004 issue, the magazine migrated from Morro Bay, California, to Port Townsend, Washington, an area with a thriving small boat community and a tradition of boat building and restoration.

By the spring of 2007, *Small Craft Advisor* became a full-color magazine, and with the May/Jun 2012, issue, it reached another milestone with its "perfect binding." That means it is not stapled and can hold its own on any magazine stand with the best periodicals.

Current wisdom in the publishing world holds that the days of the slick-covered magazine are numbered, but *Small Craft Advisor* has not only weathered this storm, but grown. Perhaps it is because Josh and Craig have held true to their original purpose and are still concerned with small seaworthy boats, and not rounding a racing mark or cruising the South Pacific. In that regard, Scamp is simply a reflection of what their magazine is all about.

Scamp's Hometown

We live in a mobile world, and if there is an image that defines us it is the automobile. As a culture, we are on the move, searching for a better job, a comfortable home, a place to raise a family, a new adventure, or a nest to retire to. The number of RVs and mobile homes on the road suggests that a gypsy gene is in our DNA. Yet, most of us harbor an image that we call "home." For the most part, it is simply there. Ask anyone where they are from, and they will most likely talk about their hometown, not where they currently live. It is not a trivial thing for it gives us definition.

In a very real sense, Scamp has a hometown where, thanks to our mobile culture, a group of creative individuals came together in a community that values wooden boats and boat building. The development of Scamp was, without doubt, driven by a fortuitous confluence of individuals in a small place—the extreme northeastern end of the Olympic Peninsula in the State of Washington where the Strait of Juan de Fuca opens into Admiralty Inlet and then Puget Sound—Port Townsend.

Some tourists follow Highway 20 and approach Port Townsend from the west. It is an easy, leisurely drive through a wooded landscape of Douglas firs, with an occasional glimpse of Discovery Bay on the left. The sign announcing the town states that the driver is entering a "Victorian Seaport and Arts Community."

Port Townsend was founded in 1851 and for forty years held the promise of becoming a major seaport. The 19th Century developers went on a building spree and constructed a new town in the ornate Victorian style, anticipating a booming commercial harbor. Then the depression of the 1890s hit and the town settled into a sleepy backwater with an occasional growth spurt, highlighted by the building of a paper mill in the 1920s. Because it was a backwater, the old Victorians were not torn down and grew old, acquiring a patina of grace and dignity.

Finally, in the 1970s, the town experienced a renaissance as new residents, mostly retirees attracted by the Victorian ambiance, moved in. It is still a small town with a population of 9,100, but it has been growing slowly over the years, thanks to tourism and many cultural events. The setting is perfect for the marine industry, too, which soon became an economic driver where designers, builders, and sailmakers could ply their trades. As you drive into town, the large boatyard on the right, along with the chandleries and related business, confirms that it is an active marine center.

Port Townsend is also served by a Washington State Ferry from Coupeville on Whidbey Island. The purist, of course, arrives by boat, preferably wooden. The stately Victorian buildings that line Water Street, the main drag, give the town a nostalgic, almost poetical air. As befits a true Victorian town, parking is at a premium. On the northern landward side of Water Street, a low bluff rises above the town and opens onto a residential area where most of the towns' folk live.

Water Street ends at another marina, also packed with boats, many of them wooden. On the right, on a point of land at the entrance to the marina, is a large two-story building, the Northwest Maritime Center. If Port Townsend is Scamp's hometown, and the Northwest Maritime Center its birthplace, then the boat shop on the ground floor was the maternity ward.

The full title of the center is the Northwest Maritime Center Wooden Boat Foundation. It is really two organizations inhabiting the same building and the organizational lines are blurry. The Executive Director, Jake Beattie, is good with that "as long as stuff happens." The Foundation runs the gift store and sponsors the annual Wooden Boat Festival in September, while the Maritime Center maintains the building, runs the boat shop, sponsors symposiums, and teaches many classes ranging from boat building to learning to sail.

The Maritime Center has been described as a "hand-to-mouth" operation, but that is not entirely true. On balance, the Center and Foundation have, in Jake's words, ". . . done a good job of securing resources for the boating community," and it is a productive relationship, witness the annual Wooden Boat show that has grown from a small affair to one of the largest of its kind in the United States.

Like many towns, Port Townsend has suffered growing pains. The Northwest School of Wooden Boat Building was founded in Port Townsend in 1981 by Bob Prothero, from Seattle. Its mission is "To teach and preserve the skills and crafts associated with fine wooden boatbuilding and other traditional arts with emphasis on the individual as a craftsperson." Unfortunately, dock and shop space was limited and the school moved to Port Hadlock, a sleepy little town one-third the size of Port Townsend, ten miles away by road.

Pete Leenhouts, the Director, takes pride in describing how the school fulfills its mission by building fifteen to seventeen boats a year, and creating a skilled group of men and women who carry the skills and crafts of the age of sail into the future. The

19

maritime links have forged a strong sense of community between the two, which is all part of Scamp's heritage.

Dreams Count

T. E. Lawrence, the real one and not the character depicted in the movie "Lawrence of Arabia," once wrote, "All men dream: but not equally." In his book, *Seven Pillars of Wisdom*, he went on to describe how dreamers ". . . may act their dream with open eyes, to make it possible."

Josh and Craig dreamed with open eyes, and, fortunately, their dream had a much a happier ending, and that is where the story of Scamp really begins. But discussing dreams in public can be a humbling, if not intimidating, endeavor. Who knows what people will think? Regardless, the two revealed their dream to the world in issue #63, May/Jun 2010:

Our own youthful dreams often featured small boats in supporting roles. Stalwart little vessels aboard which we'd venture across nebulous bodies of water in search of uncharted shores and uninhabited islands. Sometimes, we'd land and go ashore to explore or make camp, often retreating to our boats to wait out a summer storm beneath a boom tent. We'd read sea stories by oil lanterns and, on clear nights, sleep under a blanket of stars.

Curiously, these fanciful voyages never involved wrestling with a heavy mast, fussing with a smelly outboard, or being held offshore by our boat's draft. And even when we pictured whitecaps kicked up by a stout afternoon breeze, never was there a chilly capsize.

If there is a defining moment when that dream turned into reality, it was during the summer of 2009 on the Columbia 150, a cruise down the Columbia River organized by Andrew Linn. Andrew is an ex-Marine who twice sailed the Texas 200 in an eight-foot plywood box called the Puddle Duck Racer, and features later in Scamp's story, but in 2009, Andrew was busy organizing the 150-mile trip down the Columbia River that paralleled a segment of the Lewis and Clark expedition.

Sailors experienced with the Columbia know this is really the wrong way to go, and it is much better to go upstream with the strong prevailing winds. Throw in the tugs and barges, container ships, car carriers, fishermen, and windsurfers with a skateboarder mentality, and the Columbia River turns into a real challenge for small craft. It was an event tailored for *Small Craft Advisor.*

Josh debated which boat to use, and approached Dave Robertson at Gig Harbor Boat Works about borrowing one of his sixteen-foot Melonseeds, and Dave graciously agreed. The Melonseed met most of Josh's requirements: shallow, flat-bottomed, rowable, comfortable enough for a week's cruise, and able to handle the high winds and chop they would encounter. But Josh ultimately wanted more protection from the elements, and settled on his Sparrow 16 with its two-foot draft.

Later on, Josh mentioned to his crew, Chuck Leinweber from Duckworks Magazine, that he had agonized over which boat to bring, and that none seemed a perfect fit. Confine two avid small craft sailors, who happen to publish magazines about small boats, on a small sailboat for a week in the company of five other small boats, and they will talk shop and brainstorm for hours at a time.

After an epiphany, that sudden perception of the essential nature of something, Josh came back buzzing with ideas about the perfect microcruiser. He even had a name: S.C.A.M.P., for *Small Craft Advisor* Magazine Project. It was time for Josh and Craig to put their money and actions where their hearts were. They decided talk to someone they knew would have the knowledge to transform these ideas into a real vessel.

The Designer

Fully aware that they are sailors with a publishing problem, and not boat builders, much less designers, Josh and Craig needed to find a kindred soul who believed that small is better. By testing and reviewing small craft for their magazine, Josh and Craig had sorted the wheat from the chaff and knew what they wanted, but knowing what you want is a far different thing than creating it. They made a decision described in *Small Craft Advisor* (issue #63):

Trying our best to distill small-boat cruising to its essence, we sorted out our ideas and took the best of them to one of our favorite designers – John Welsford. It shouldn't have surprised us that, being of a like mind, he responded enthusiastically.

What we commissioned was the most micro of cruisers. We wanted a cabin, not for a claustrophobic casket-like berth – but for dry storage, buoyancy, and a bulwark against wind and seas. We tried to be honest about the compromises. In describing the boat to John we said Scamp would be so small that, "the designer himself might cringe a little when he puts the pencil down."

Their choice was a good one.

John Welsford does not fit the image of a designer sitting behind a drafting table with a sharpened pencil in hand. The Kiwi is in his early sixties, and at five-foot nine-inches tall with brown eyes, salt and pepper hair, and neatly trimmed beard and moustache, looks more ready to play a role in a remake of Captains' Courageous. His droll and quick humor are in the best tradition of any New Zealand pub, and if something breaks down or needs fixing, you definitely want to let John do it.

When asked about his education and training as a boat designer, John replied that his only qualification is "my driver's license." He then quickly points out that he suffers from "a mild case of "disnumeracy." A quick check of the dictionary for a definition of the word proved fruitless, and that led to a search on Google. The only word close is "innumeracy," or the inability to handle fundamental mathematics like addition and subtraction. Yet, John uses more numbers in small boat design than most, so let the reader beware—John will have you on in a heartbeat.

But when it comes to designing a boat, John is all business, and he was on the same page as Josh and Craig from the very start. Perhaps, John said it best in *Small Craft Advisor* (issue #37):

I love small blue water cruisers. I read everything I can get my hands on about successful voyages in small boats . . . . There is something endearing about a very small cruiser. The easily handled rig, the cozy cabin – cute, approachable, and affordable. The latter is a large part of the attraction! To sit in traffic every day, coughing in the fumes of the big truck ahead, with the prospect of many similar days to come is not good for the soul. The conventional ethic suggests that it takes a quarter of a million dollars to buy a boat capable of going anywhere up the coast on a fine day. Not so. The thought of something that can be built and outfitted within a small budget is very appealing when driving home from being chewed out by the boss!

When designing a boat, John first develops a 'brief." What exactly does the customer want? In many respects, it is an education for skipper and designer. He evaluates the environment with an emphasis on climate. What will the boat be used for? What are the customer's real needs? What are the resources available for the build? How will it be kept and maintained?

He works to distill the project to its basics, and it boils down to pages of numbers that detail the ballast ratio, sail area to displacement, prismatic coefficient, block coefficient, etc. John knows the customer is convinced when they are in the same place, and what he envisions matches the customer's needs. He builds from there, and, being practical, he adheres to a basic rule of seamanship in his designs: Keep the water out.

John has been actively designing boats for nearly thirty years, and has built twenty-six over that time. With each project, he has added to his considerable bag of tools, and the words "affordable, achievable, safe, and comfortable" are key to his design philosophy. He smiles when he says, "When you commission a design, you are buying a truckload of experience." He tells how he became involved with Scamp in issue #63 of *Small Craft Advisor.*

I've been corresponding with Joshua Colvin and Craig Wagner, editors of this esteemed publication, for a few years now, and have written articles and design features for quite a few years . . . Knowing their bias to the small and simple I was not at all surprised to hear from them asking if a very small cruiser might be a practical proposition . . . That is an area of boating that is very close to my heart. . . . "Ten feet long," they e-mailed. "Sleep on board for a weekend. Something that would daysail an adult and a couple of children. Really easy to build in a garage, and small enough to not need an expensive trailer or a big car to tow it."

For John, Scamp was the perfect commission, and would prove to be the fourth in a series of three dinghies he had designed; Tender Behind at 7-feet 2-inches, Sherpa at 9-feet 6-inches, and Tread Lightly at 13-feet. Of the three, Sherpa was the closest in concept with a pram bow and good hull form for stability and load carrying. After exchanging e-mails, what emerged was:

. . . . a tad over 10 feet long and a whisker under five-feet wide – she is short and fat. With her water ballast she will be exceptionally stable allowing the skipper to move around the little ship without worrying about falling out. Scamp has plenty freeboard, lots of dry storage, a self draining cockpit and for safety's sake, a huge amount of air-tank buoyancy. . . That little "cabin" is really a secure locker and buoyancy air tank. There is room for a sleeping bag, dry clothes, food, matches and such. There is also space for a lot more stores and equipment under the side seats, and if the skipper is intending to get away for a really big adventure, there is more space under the cockpit floor.

That self draining floor is the bunk, wide enough for shoulders, long enough for all but the tallest NBA player, sheltered and secure with their head up under the after end of the "cabin." . . . . The centerboard is hidden on the starboard side seat front, and does not get in the way at all. The asymmetry making such a tiny difference that few will ever notice from one tack to the other. . . . With twin skegs under her flat bottom, and a kickup rudder, she can sneak into very shallow water, and will sit upright when the tide goes out, often an ideal way of spending a night out in a small boat that would otherwise be bounced around by the waves and power boat wakes in a big boat anchorage.

The rig is a simple balanced lugsail. I'd expect the boat to be ready to launch within 15 minutes of arrival at the boat ramp, the mast being unstayed and light enough to just pick up and plug in, the yard and boom with the sail being easy to fit, leaving only the rudder to hang on.

John admits that at 10-feet 4-inches, Scamp was a really tight design, and while a six-foot tall skipper could sail the boat, he would not be 100% comfortable. However, Scamp was to experience growing pains that would delight both the dreamers and the designer. But that was in the future and part of this story.

Looking back, John believes that Scamp may be his most successful design—to date. "What I designed was a big cockpit and left the rest of the boat out." That is a typical Welsfordian understatement as the small craft incorporates many sophisticated design elements yet only requires moderate building skills to construct. And, at the same time, it remains a very approachable boat for skippers and non-sailors. Just watch people around the little craft, and there is no doubt as to its appeal. It is worth noting that John's wife, Denny, who is not a sailor, wants one. Experience would prove that John got the yin and yang right.

Building the Prototype

Josh and Craig introduced Scamp to the world in issue #63 of their magazine. There it was for everyone to see: the dream of a small boat complete with a line drawing of a pram-bowed, ten-foot four-inch dinghy with a balanced lug rigged sail. Comments and opinions flew fast and furious from the very first. Steve Haines, who has been mistaken for a refugee from a Hemmingway like-alike contest, was enchanted from the very first and wanted to build one. But a quick study of the plans revealed that would take some doing.

Josh approached the Northwest School of Boat Building in Port Hadlock with a deal: if they would build a Scamp in one of their classes, he and Craig would furnish the materials and provide ad space in *Small Craft Advisor* for the school. The school loved the boat and agreed to it, but because of commitments and scheduling conflicts, couldn't start until the next year, 2011. Later, at a small-boat-get-together in Port Townsend, Josh mentioned the arrangement to Kees Prins, the boat shop manager/educator at the Northwest Maritime Center. Kees considered the project and said, "We could build it for you at the Maritime Center."

Josh simply says, "That's how it got going." But that is another classic understatement. Because of that decision, three individuals became involved with Scamp—Kees Prins, Brandon Davis, and the Boatologist—who were critical in the small craft's development. Each played a different role, but it was Kees who took the lead.

When asked why he is so attracted to small sailboats, Kees Prins gazed out the window with a soft and far-away look as he reached back into memory. "The seeds were planted early," he replied with a slightly accented, but perfect command of the English language. If you listen carefully, you can even hear the commas and periods in his grammatically correct conversation.

Kees, pronounced "Case, like in Case tractor" as he politely corrects a mispronunciation, is a transplanted Dutchman in his fifties, with dark-blond shaggy curly hair, blue eyes, and a short and well-trimmed beard with wisps of gray. At five foot ten, he looks Dutch, and talks with the same thoughtful consideration this writer learned to appreciate from his Dutch neighbors when he lived in the Netherlands.

Kees is a graduate of the Dutch educational system, which makes ours look anemic in comparison, and originally studied biology at Leiden University. But he soon gravitated away from the abstract intellectual into the real world of carpentry and restoring old windmills. Later, he studied design as he added to his boatbuilding skills, but he has always had a penchant for teaching. In 1996, he and his wife established a boatbuilding school in Holland, and over the course of six years, taught 350 students who built forty boats.

In answering the "why" of small craft addiction, he talked about growing up in a family with a fifteen-foot, mahogany keelboat. The simplicity and functionality of the boat made a lasting impression, and when he was in his twenties, he acquired it and sailed through Holland on the canals and rivers, and waterways. But the attraction became fixed when he found a Drascombe. There was something deeply appealing about the boat, and when he immigrated to the States, he bought a fifteen-foot Dabber. Kees sailed the boat for six years before returning to Holland in 1996 to establish the Boatbuilding School.

Naturally, he took the boat with him. He sailed the Drascombe for another six years in Holland before he returned to the States with his family to settle in Port Townsend, Washington. Again, he took the boat with him. It was also in Port Townsend where he met Josh Colvin.

There is a little of the wanderer in Kees, but he has a strong sense of place, which helps explain his attachment to building homes. But his first love is building and designing small boats, and he found a home in the Northwest Maritime Center in Port Townsend as the Boat Shop Educator. There, his skills at carpentry and boat building melded with design and education, which is one of the reasons that Josh was pleased to have Kees build the prototype. Kees immediately went to work, lofting and cutting templates. He made small changes, tweaking and improving the design, and early on knew that the real answer was to create a kit and assemble that.

He had just the man in mind, Brandon Davis of Turn Point Design.

The CNC Operator

One of the marvels of the computer age is CNC, or Computer Numerical Control, by which machine tools are controlled by computer programs. Numerical control has revolutionized the machining process, and, combined with CAD (Computer Aided Design) programs, the entire design and machine production industry has been transformed. At one time, what started as a dream and took form in a design depended on the machinist and craftsman to become reality. It was a very difficult process, and the final product was often flawed or required modification.

The evolution of the automobile is a prime example and gave a whole new meaning to the term "lemon." CAD now gives the designer the capability to preview and test and change the parameters of a design before entering production, minimizing the probability of creating, and then disposing, of a flawed product.

Once the design is refined, CNC allows the designer/operator to link the computer to a router that machines the final product. Instead of a machinist turning the wheels and dials of a lathe or feeding a cutter, the computer does the work and creates a finished product.

Brandon Davis is the owner and CNC operator of Turn Point Design, and has been active in the marine trades industry for over twenty years. Friendly and personable, he spends much of his time in front of a computer. Originally from Seattle, he settled in Friday Harbor in the San Juan Islands where he opened a boat business. Later, he gravitated to Port Townsend and started Turn Point Design. Most of Turn Point's work is mold and tooling related, and Brandon created the rudder mold and daggerboards used by New Zealand's Oracle team to win the thirty-third America's Cup.

Turn Point also manufactures hydrofoils, daggerboards, and rudders for the International Fourteen, one of the world's premier sailing classes. Thanks to class rules, the dinghy, or skiff, is on the edge of sailing technology. It is an absolute hot rod that continues to challenge small craft skippers and pushes the design of small boat technology, and Turn Point is part of that legacy.

Beside parts for the International Fourteen, they have machined over 150 tools and 1200 parts, including fixtures, museum displays, signs, post machined laminated parts, foam inserts for foils, aluminum honeycomb, and the list goes on—including precision-cut marine plywood kits for small boats. Turn Point's shop space in Port Townsend is 5000 square feet in size, but its impact is impressive and far-reaching.

Brandon was in New Zealand working with Oracle on an America's Cup contender when Kees contacted him about the Scamp. A steady stream of messages linked them, and the project was soon underway.

Design into Reality

Kees and Brandon worked well together, and Kees knew Brandon could create a computer-cut kit with his automated router that would be extremely efficient and accurate. Josh immediately bought into the project.

From the very first, Kees and Brandon felt that the ten-foot Scamp envisioned by Josh and John was too small. CAD programs facilitate comparisons, so Brandon enlarged the design to fourteen feet and inserted a proportionally sized human figure. It was too big, and the enlargement would have meant redesigning the Scamp altogether.

Kees suggested reducing the size to twelve feet. Josh studied it, liked what he saw, and suggested they make it eleven foot – eleven inches in length. Josh contacted John Welsford, who readily agreed it made for a better boat. Not only was the Scamp twenty percent bigger, its stability had substantially increased, which made for a far more capable boat when the winds rise.

Scamp was a go.

In short order, a stack of computer-cut marine-grade plywood parts appeared on the floor of the maritime center. Kees drafted Scott Jones and Sarah Rudolph, both employed at the Maritime Center, to do the actual construction. It was a fortunate choice as Sarah had also studied at the International Yacht Restoration School in Rhode Island, and Scott at the Northwest School of Wooden Boat Building in Port Hadlock.

Make no mistake, Kees is a very hands-on educator and they formed a skillful team when they started construction in early September 2010, which coincided with the Port Townsend Wooden Boat Festival. It was the prototype's introduction to the public and it was an instant attraction.

During construction, there was a constant exchange between Scott, Sarah, Kees, Josh, and Brandon as they refined the design. They altered the cabin top slightly and positioned hatches for access as they bent, adjusted, and cut, working to get the fit and shapes right. At the same time, Brandon developed ways for the kit components to self-align with slots and tabs.

There were other issues to address, namely the spars, rigging, and writing of a construction manual. The latter would take another set of skills, where a sharp eye for detail and a sense of classification blended with a photographer's eye and the ability to describe a construction process with literary skills. Fortunately, there was just such an individual in Port Townsend.

The Boatologist

Just about everyone who served in the military ran into, often out of necessity, the Radar O'Reilly characterized in TV's "Mash." In reality, they are a mixed bag of characters, usually a mid-ranked sergeant or officer. Some are sneaky and worldly, some almost saintly, others are laid back with a wicked sense of humor.

But they really do exist and serve a very useful purpose. They know how to make the system work and are always there when it really gets tough. They can find the indispensable part to fix a broken airframe, know the right secretary in the right office to get the right signature on a requisition form, can make end runs around immovable commanders, and have an institutional memory that tells the real story. They are a rare combination of lubricant and glue that makes it all work.

Luckily, Scamp has its own Radar O'Reilly—The boatologist.

Simeon Baldwin does not look like a Radar O'Reilly. In his late sixties, he's tall and lanky with salt and pepper hair, and hazel eyes. Simeon is pleasant, laid back, and quick to smile, which may explain why he has been happily married for over forty years. He grew up in the Far East, mostly in Hong Kong, and started sailing at a young age, mainly in fourteen-foot Redwing dinghies and was still a teenager when he first experienced blue water sailing.

Later, he attended Stanford University where he majored in marine biology. After graduating, he entered the Navy and became a pilot, flying EC-121s, the military version of the three-tailed Lockheed Constellation. Given the aircraft's dolphin-shaped fuselage, it can be assumed there was a connection to his major while at Stanford.

After retiring from the Navy, Simeon and his wife eventually settled in Port Ludlow, some twenty miles south of Port Townsend, where he became the flotilla commander of the local Coast Guard Auxiliary. Wanting to get closer to the water, he built a Pygmy kayak in 2007. One paddle led to another, and he found that happy spot between the high-flying Navy aviator and the submerged marine biologist.

Eventually, Simeon made the acquaintance of Kees at the Northwest Maritime Center, where he volunteered to help build a nineteen-foot yawl. It wasn't long before his skills at finding the needed oddball part, the right-sized washer, or the rare whatever-you-call-it surfaced. He was always there, helping when needed and cheering everyone on.

Like many at the Maritime Center, Simeon was intrigued by Scamp from the very first and wanted to get involved. He volunteered to help Scott and Sarah as they labored over the prototype, and spent hours filling, epoxying, and sanding, not the easiest task, but an essential one. Then he started taking photos, a perfect blend with his prior experience developing technical manuals for the Navy and his education as a marine biologist where he had learned to classify and document everything.

Kees recognized an opportunity and suggested to Josh that he approach Simeon with an offer to write the build manual. Josh has described Simeon as "The gamest guy I know," and made Simeon an offer too good to refuse: If Simeon would write the build manual, SCA would spring for a Scamp kit. Simeon accepted, and the result was a hundred-page manual that far exceeds the build manuals this writer has used. Nevertheless, Simeon treats it as a work in progress and is continuing to improve it.

Should the reader ever wander into the Maritime Center, they might miss Simeon, but if they start to build a small craft in the boat shop he will be there, quietly helping, because that's what boatologists do.

Reaching an End

While Simeon started to work writing the build manual, Kees, Scott, and Sarah pressed ahead with the prototype. It was much more than just assembling a kit as the pieces came from Turn Point Design, but a process of constant feedback and refinement. The effort resulted in what Scott describes as "A high-class kit."

But there was much more to be done, and Kees led the effort in creating spars and rigging. He started by designing the hollow wooden mast, making it light, yet strong. He smiles when he evaluates the result. "Some bending is actually good." He remembers it as being a challenging time, but the melding of skills, experience, and attitudes resulted in a well-constructed and successful design. How well-constructed and successful would require the test of time.

The Scamp is not a simple kit to build; it requires moderate building skills, and, as Brandon Davis points out, "It takes time and commitment." Yet, the team finished the prototype in six weeks, just in time for the arrival of the test pilot.

Photo: Debra Colvin

Creating Scamp
Scott Jones and Sarah Randolph making magic in the boat shop

The Test Pilot

Many geographic locales and arenas of human endeavor—intellectual, economic, athletic—have resident personalities, living or dead, who give life and character to the subject. Philosophy has its Socrates, the business world has Henry Ford, baseball has Babe Ruth, Colorado Alferd E. Packer, aviation Amelia Earhard, and the small world of microcruisers has Howard Rice.

These very different people in very different fields share a common trait—they push things to the limit. There is a risk in that, and a taste of hemlock or length of hemp may occasionally be in the offing—just ask Socrates or Alferd—or you can get horribly lost like poor Amelia.

Fortunately, Howard Rice has avoided the consequences associated with being on the cutting edge, perhaps because he has an exquisite sense of balance and direction. At five-feet eleven-inches tall, with brown hair, and hazel eyes, Howard is very fit, and although he claims to be in his late fifties, can easily pass for fifteen years younger; the fact that he has been a strict vegetarian since he was twenty-two may be a factor.

Although he might blush at the suggestion, there is a touch of the Renaissance Man about Howard. He is an adventurer, environmentalist, a peripatetic citizen of the world living in Micronesia and Japan with this wife Keiko. Howard has been known to philosophize, and has a style of writing almost Edwardian in tone. Moreover, he is a confirmed small craft sailor, who, at the time this was written, owned thirty-seven small sailboats.

Howard's passion for small boats started when he was a teenager and acquired a Cape Dory Typhoon. Although he has flirted with larger boats, he has always focused on his true love, small sailing canoes and microcruisers. That love, combined with an adventurous spirit, led to an epic quest to round Cape Horn at the southern tip of Chile.

The Horn is rightfully infamous as one of the most dangerous capes in the world, and Howard decided to do it in a 15-foot Klepper sailing canoe. His planning and preparation paid off when he doubled the Cape (going both ways) from December 1989 to March 1990. Later, he settled in Micronesia where he worked for the governor of the State of Pohnepi and was instrumental in creating the World Park. The locale was also perfect for pursuing his love affair with small blue-water sailing craft.

It was only natural that he should make the acquaintance of John Welsford, and, much later, Josh Colvin. Always looking for the "perfect microcruiser," the initial design of the Scamp caught his attention. But at 10-foot 4-inches in length, he just "didn't get the boat." When he saw the 11-foot-11-inch version, he knew he had found the microcruiser he was looking for. There is a saying in the aviation community that if an aircraft looks right, it is right. It is an intuitive reaction, and he immediately told Josh, "I'm buying two."

Now he had to get his hands on one to validate his decision.

Howard tells the story in the article "SCAMP Evaluation" in issue #68 of *Small Craft Advisor*. Howard e-mailed Josh that he hoped to drop by Port Townsend to take a look and talk about the new boat. After an extensive correspondence, Josh offered the Scamp for a test cruise and organized the required gear.

Howard arrived in Port Townsend on December 29, 2010, to gray and threatening weather. The next day, he met Scamp and liked what he saw. Evaluating the conditions, Howard decided to test the boat on challenging seas. There was some risk, but Josh was confident that Howard could safely wring out the Scamp and bring her home.

What transpired is not recommended for the average skipper. After a brief shakedown, Howard headed for Mystery Bay on Marrowstone Island, five miles away, in the late afternoon. He immediately encountered eight to ten knot winds and the boat sailed perfectly. But conditions were becoming more difficult as night fell; he made the inlet to Kilisut Harbor between Marrowstone and Indian Island, and decided to anchor off Indian Island as the winds rose and the temperature fell. After a night that involved hauling anchor and relocating to a less exposed anchorage, he made for Mystery Bay before heading back to Port Townsend in freezing conditions.

It was so cold that Howard did not chance removing a glove to adjust the GPS, but believed he had the small craft up to between five and six knots. "I had a great romping sail of long tacks to weather across open water to Port Townsend, finally ending the day in ghosting conditions in the lee along the storefronts of town as the second day's sunset blazed red behind the snow capped peaks. I did not want to come back." Perhaps no better tribute can be paid to the designer and builders.

Howard acknowledged Scamp was a work in progress and he saw the need for more tests and development, but his evaluation was unequivocal and he gave it close to a perfect ten across the board. He had found the microcruiser he was looking for and made a promise. "In fact, I hope to be involved in the development of Scamp from here forward." It was a promise he would keep.

In March of 2011, Howard returned to Port Townsend for extensive capsize tests. It was cold and windy as he put the small craft through the wringer, and the event was posted on YouTube. He discovered that the boat is difficult to capsize and easily righted; further, once back on its bottom, it won't sail away and leave the skipper in the water.

Photo: Debra Colvin
Getting ready
Howard Rice topping off the water ballast

Better still, when back in the boat, the skipper can sail away without bailing. Scamp can be set up for a high-side recovery when it is on its side, but the skipper has to be careful not to let the water ballast box get past center or the boat might turn turtle. He concluded that it is much better just to go with it, go into the water, move around to the bottom, and pull the boat upright.

He would later demonstrate the technique at the first Small Craft Skills Academy, and, in August of 2012, he would again return to Port Townsend for the first Scamp Camp where he, John Welsford, and Scott Jones would lead thirteen builders through the process of building ten kit boats at the same time on the floor of the Northwest Maritime Center.

But that is a story for later telling and much had to happen first.

Photo: Debra Colvin
Shake Down
Howard Rice (helm) and Russell Brown sailing Scamp
during capsize testing

THREE

The Builders

Building Scamp

By December 2010, all the basics were in place. The design had been expanded and refined, plans drafted and printed, a kit was in production, and the prototype built. Equally important, the prototype had passed it's first tests with flying colors. But could Scamp make a successful transition to the public? Could an amateur boat builder turn the plans into reality in a workshop without falling on his wood chisel and doing pushups in frustration? Could the skipper with average building skills actually assemble the kit in a garage working independently and relying on the build manual?

And the big question was still out there—how well would a home-built Scamp perform on the water in the hands of the average skipper? Finally, was a fiberglass version possible?

For better or worse, a fiberglass version of a small boat is critical, otherwise, it may, at best, remain a "cult boat" with a small but loyal following. The vast majority of small craft sailors are not builders, nor do they have the desire to adopt a wooden boat and devote the time and effort to maintaining it; they simply want to be on the water quickly, with a minimum of fuss. Josh and Craig were fully aware of this and Josh was working the problem.

The first set of plans had gone out to Mike Monies in Eufaula, Oklahoma. Mike is a very focused builder and he set to work building two Scamps for the upcoming Everglades Challenge in March of 2011—a major undertaking. At the same time, Josh was looking for someone to build the first official kit boat at the Northwest Maritime Center. He found the builder he was looking for, and on December 2, 2010, the most scampish of skippers— a storied man with a purposeful twinkle in his eye—arrived from Fort Bragg, California.

Building the *B. Frank*

Dan Phy is an avid small craft skipper who is always open to suggestion when boats are involved. Just mention a faraway sailing venture and Dan lights up like the alarm bells at a fire station. Dan is a retired firefighter, and that could just be an ingrained reaction. Add an understanding wife who sends him off with "Have a good time and don't kill yourself," and Dan is hooking up the trailer in short order.

Besides having a wanderlust, Dan has a bucket list, and had wanted to attend the boat building class at the Northwest Maritime Center since he first heard about it.

Dan is a robust, active skipper with blue eyes and gray hair, and at five-foot nine-inches, in excellent shape. Born and raised in Venice, California, he first started sailing when he was fifteen. For a time, he lived on a small wooden sailboat, but turned to happy domesticity at twenty-eight when he married and started a family. After retiring from the Los Angeles Fire Department, he built on his skills as an emergency medical technician and became a surgical nurse in Fort Bragg, California. Dan's travails in the operating room make for many entertaining dock parties, but that is another story. After years of kayaking and camping, he bought another sailboat—a West Wight Potter fifteen.

Interviewing Dan is like sailing in Force Five winds—it is a sporting endeavor. He is a superb raconteur, but occasionally he cuts to the quick. When asked why he sails small craft, he simply says, "They are fun. You use them." One of the conceits of small craft sailors is that they are on the water actually building tiller time while bigger craft remain tied up at the dock gathering barnacles and moss.

For proof, they point to the forest of masts languishing in marinas. But there are also many small boats hiding in barns, garages, backyards that never see the water. They are simply hidden out of sight while the bigger members of their family make for great photo opportunities. For Dan, it is not really a question of size, but being on the water in a small boat makes for outrageous adventures. With that in mind, he has experimented with a series of craft, and still owns three boats and four kayaks.

Currently, his main boat is a much-modified Montgomery 15. When asked about the size of his mini-fleet, a wistful look spreads across Dan's face, and he mumbles something about there being two empty spaces in his barn. For most of 2011, the first kit-built Scamp resided there. How it got there is a serendipitous blend of circumstance and Dan's wanderlust that would make him a key player in the Scamp story.

Dan was visiting Steve Haines, an old friend, in September of 2010 with the intention of sailing on the nearby Kentucky Lakes. At the time, Josh and Craig were using Steve as a sounding board, bouncing the concept of Scamp and the first drawings from John Welsford off him. Like a good host, Steve shared the bouncings with Dan, who was immediately intrigued. There was something in the lines of the sturdy little microcruiser that touched the small-craft sailor in Dan. Steve was equally smitten.

Not long after returning to Fort Bragg, and two weeks before the next boat-building class started in December 2010, Josh called Dan. According to Dan, they were looking for a "crazy SOB" to build the first of three official kit boats at the Maritime Center. Given Dan's love of small boats, it was a slam dunk, and he was quickly loading his camper.

When Dan arrived at the Northwest Maritime Center on December 2, 2010—a Thursday—Scott Jones and Sarah Rudolph had just finished the prototype, and it was sitting in the corner of the workshop. Dan was disappointed to learn that the projected three boats for construction were now down to one; on the good side, that meant he would get a lot of attention, help, and kibitzing.

Looking back, Dan calculates that he actually worked alone perhaps twenty percent of the time, a good thing as the Scamp is a time-consuming boat to build. Dan admits that he didn't know what was involved and seriously underestimated the time and effort required. He estimates that he spent nine to fifteen hours a day with a short lunch break during the sixteen days he was building Scamp # 6.

There was no construction manual, but Kees had arranged for Simeon Baldwin to write the manual as he built his boat. Fortunately, Dan was building his boat at the same time that Simeon developed the manual. There was a great deal of interaction between Dan, Kees, and Simeon as Dan built the first kit boat.

Early on, Dan realized that he needed help and enlisted Scott and Sarah to construct the mast, boom and yard. Building the mast out of eight separate pieces was a group effort from the very first, and Dan recalls his near heart attack when they "tested" the mast. The veteran builders laid the mast between two sawhorses, rigged a strap in the middle, and started hanging dumb bells from the strap to measure the deflection. Dan breathed a sigh of relief when they stopped at 220 pounds. The strong practical streak in Dan realized he was onto a good thing, and he commissioned the Maritime Center to also build the centerboard and rudder. Again, Kees was involved and he worked with Simeon to shape and refine the centerboard.

Without doubt, Kees Prins was a major force in bringing Dan's Scamp to completion. There was a bad moment when Dan tired to attach the first plank up from the flat bottom. It didn't fit. Dan recalls Kees "sweating blood for thirty to forty minutes solving the problem." The planks had been mismarked and were 180 degrees out. Recounting the story makes the solution seem easy, but Dan doesn't remember it being that way. Another glitch came when Dan tried to fit the cabin to the hull; there was a big gap at the bottom, and again, Kees solved the problem.

Dan has two overwhelming memories of his time at the Maritime Center: fiberglassing and sanding. Everything was triple-coated in epoxy and sanding took on a life of its own. And Kees made sure Dan did it right. Kees insisted that every part be dry fitted until it was ready to be epoxied into place. They paid special attention to the centerboard trunk and the water ballast tank, which had to be solid and watertight before it received the requisite three coats of epoxy. When the wire stitches that tied the parts together were removed, Kees insisted that hardwood toothpicks be glued in the holes before fiberglassing them over. Dan protested that it was unnecessary as fiberglassing would do the job. Kees ended the discussion with "Not at this school."

The attention to detail was fantastic. It was a collegial effort and Scamp acted as a magnet, drawing in everyone at the Maritime Center. Dan recalls Josh frequently wandering in, a quiet observer watching his child grow and develop. Perhaps the best testimonial to their accomplishment is the photo of the unfinished Scamp loaded on its trailer for the trip to Fort Bragg. A great deal of work remained to he done, but the big smile on Dan's face leaves little doubt that the Scamp would be finished, and finished well.

Safely back in Fort Bragg, Dan was to rediscover a basic truth about boatbuilding—the devil is in the details. Looking back, Dan estimates that the boat was approximately half finished when he pushed it into his workshop area. Even though Scamp is less than twelve-feet long, a one-car garage is cramped. Building the Scamp was proving much more difficult than he had anticipated; fortunately, Dan had previously built two boats, a kayak and a sailing pram, and had a good friend, Jim Kirwan, there to help.

Photo: Dan Phy

The *B. Frank* Heads Home
(l to r): Dan Phy, Kees Prins, Simeon Baldwin

Without a builder's manual to guide him, Dan worked through the finishing process, solving one problem at a time. Kees Prins had given him a handwritten list of things to do with detailed instructions outlined on notebook paper, and that helped immensely. Kees and Simeon Baldwin were only a phone call away, too, and both gave unsparingly of their time when Dan called with a problem.

Dan recalls the time and effort it took them just to insert the bolt for the centerboard pin. It was a very close fit and difficult to align, but with a healthy vocabulary and perseverance, Dan and Jim succeeded. Dan recalls the biggest speed bump in the finishing process was ". . . worrying about the unknowns. Don't screw it up now."

E-mails and postings on the Trailer Sailor Bulletin Board whetted the interest of the Northern California microcruiser crowd, and a christening was set for mid June, if Dan could finish the Scamp in time. The story is in issue #73 of *Small Craft Advisor* by this writer:

Three of the hardcore skippers of the Potter Yachters of Northern California, aka 'All the Usual Suspects,' were milling around the Oakland Yacht Club in Alameda, California, in eager anticipation of Dan Phy's arrival. Normally, the Suspects function on Potter Standard Time where calendars are more important than watches, but June 14, 2011, was different. Dan was towing his home-built Scamp, the only one in captivity in California. Rumor had it that it was not only the first kit-built model, but the third hull ever launched.

But Dan was late. He was driving down from Fort Bragg with his loyal sidekick, Jim Kirwan, and they were stopping at every chandlery and West Marine on the way in search of bits and pieces to complete the rigging. Dan wanted a snappy, sharp, sailable Scamp for the christening on the next day. Being a Potter, he expected to hear "What a cute little boat!" but he needed one that would impress them on the water, hopefully with a view of its cute little stern. The Suspects are an optimistic lot.

By mid afternoon, the soon-to-be christened Scamp was tied to the guest dock and appropriate comments were heard; however, there were an amazing amount of technical questions Dan was obliged to answer. Finally, Don Person, the intrepid Council of Elder (C of E) of the Nautical Order of Geezers, arrived. A hard silence came down as Dan awaited the verdict of the elder NOG. The august personage studied the Scamp with a critical eye and pronounced judgment: "That's a neat little boat."

Following another round of gentle harassment, Dan stretched a Bikini-sized tarp over the boom for a tent and all repaired in good order to Jim Kirwan's able craft for Happy Hour. It was an unusually warm evening with soft breezes and a gorgeous sunset, all harbingers of the next day. And the booze was excellent. After much discussion, it was decided a gourmet dinner was called for and they headed for the local Subway sandwich shop. Back at the dock, four skippers climbed aboard their sturdy micro cruisers to bed down for the night, keeping a watchful eye on Dan to see if he could really stretch out and sleep in the Scamp's cockpit. He did.

The evening's promise held true and Wednesday's dawn was magnificent. The Suspects gathered for coffee in the Oakland Yacht Club's meeting room before driving to Jim's, a local eatery with lumberjack-sized breakfasts, excellent coffee, and friendly waitresses. After solving the world's problems, it was time to attend to the business of the day. The original plan called for the christening to take place at the Grand Street Ramp in Alameda, but construction work on the dock precluded the somber ambiance a christening requires. A decision was made and the growing flock of Potters flocked back to the guest dock at the Oakland Yacht Club. Dory Taylor, a founder of the Potter Yachters, studied the Scamp and gazed wistfully into the past. He had seen a lot of boats and water pass under the bridge. He gave a little nod and said, "I love it." Harry Gordon, another Potter plankowner, could only agree.

Amazingly, twenty Potters were gathered on the dock at the appointed time (see above remarks about Potter Standard Time). The C of E took command and called for order. He asked Dan to share a few words about the Scamp's history and construction before allowing a few questions and answers. Then, drawing himself to his full five-feet-four and a quarter, the C of E commenced the christening. "Ahoy all ye Ladies, Shipmates, Able Seamen, Scalawags, Miscreants, Potters, and assorted NOGs. Gather 'round and heed these words." Not a tear was seen as the twenty assembled Potters raised their glasses for the appropriate toasts to the *B. Frank*. With the ceremony duly completed, the assemblage meandered into the club's dining room for lunch on Dan.

A topic of conversation was why Dan had chosen to name the *B. Frank* after SCA's columnist and resident scalawag, B. Frank Franklin. Dan muttered some excuse about losing a bet in some shady saloon, all befitting the modus operandi of B.F.F. In order to avoid further controversy, the C of E exercised his authority and granted " . . . a full, free, and absolute pardon unto B. Frank Franklin for all offenses against humanity and journalism." With the issue settled and the name *B. Frank* granted legitimacy, it was time to see how well the little vessel sailed.

A small fleet of Potters followed Dan in the *B. Frank* onto the Oakland Estuary for its maiden sail. It was a photo moment that would have made Kodak proud. Back at the dock, Dan tried to play it cool and spoke of good hull speed and being responsive to a light helm. But his big grin said it all. Happy Hour that evening on the dock was filled with compliments and admiration for the *B. Frank*.

The wind was kicking up on Thursday, and Jim Kirwan suggested the Suspects sail across San Francisco Bay to South Beach next to the Golden Gate Bridge for lunch. Five boats accompanied the *B. Frank* as Dan poked its bow into the Bay. The combination of wind and choppy, confused water was enough to stir thoughts of reefing, but the stalwart fleet pressed on and the *B. Frank* proved it was a spirited performer. After lunch, Dan set a reef before casting off. While the conditions back were sporting at times, the B. Frank showed her stuff and arrived safely back under full sail. Dan was now certain he had a winner.

As for the rest of us? Well, I want one.

The last sentence of the above article was to prove prophetic for this writer.

Dan had spent over six months laboring on the *B. Frank*, and is justifiably proud of what he built. It is a sturdy little boat built in the best traditions of the Northwest Maritime Center, and it shows the attention to detail that Kees Prins demands. When asked to evaluate the Scamp, Dan grew serious. "On reflection, Scamp at eleven-feet eleven-inches defies mathematical doctrine in a number of ways. First, the 'fun quotient' of building and sailing Scamp is far greater than eleven-feet eleven-eleven inches. Second, the sum of Scamp is far more than the approximate 198 pieces included in the kit. Third, Scamp sails faster and better than it should at eleven-eleven. Fourth, Scamp is the most durable, recoverable camp cruiser that I know of."

Then he gets to the heart of the matter. "In summation, I like Scamp!" Dan may not be a theoretical mathematician, but he got the sums right.

The Tale of the Red Scamp

While Dan Phy was laboring over the *B. Frank* on the West Coast, a plans-built Scamp was coming to life some 1500 miles away in Eufaula, Oklahoma.

Conventional wisdom in the small craft community holds that there are two kinds of boat people—those who build boats, and those who sail them. Mike Monies, in his good-natured, down-home, friendly way, challenges that belief. Not only does Mike build a variety of boats, he builds them fast and well. While he builds to plans, he constantly makes small changes and modifications, creating no-frills, solid boats meant to be sailed in a variety of conditions.

Mike describes himself as a "Transplanted Texan living in exile in Oklahoma" although he was born in Los Angeles. He now lives near Lake Eufaula, the tenth largest manmade lake in the United States. Mike and his wife, Jackie, are the organizers of Sail Oklahoma, a messabout which brings around a hundred small craft of all descriptions together every October for four days. Mike is in his mid sixties, and at five-foot eight, is physically fit. He and Jackie have been married over forty years and have two daughters, who Mike laughingly blames for causing his gray hair. Jackie loves to sail, and, at one time, they owned a boat brokerage in Houston, Texas. While Mike writes a column for *Small Craft Advisor*, Jackie handles the correspondence, freeing up time for Mike to build boats.

Mike's love affair with small sailboats started when he was eight and saw a rubber inner tube with a sail in Popular Science. He built one and immediately tested it. Fortunately, the wind was on-shore, keeping him safe. From there, he went on to build a dinghy with his father. The die was cast and he's been building and sailing boats ever since. After he and Jackie married, he built a twenty-one foot cat-ketch sharpie in the late 1970s. Like so many skippers, he kept thinking bigger, and in 1985 built a thirty-two foot Ted Brewer designed Lazy Jack from a fiberglass hull and deck kit. He soon discovered that he was spending more time varnishing than sailing and that cured him of big-boat fever.

He sold the Lazy Jack and never looked back. Mike did run into the Lazy Jack in May 2012. Much of it was still original, a tribute to his building skills.

The 2009 Texas 200, a cruise modeled after the Everglades Challenge but not so challenging, caught Mike's attention. Naturally, he built a boat to participate, an eleven-foot six-inch Phil Bolger Cartopper. The Cartopper is a good-looking boat with traditional lines and a reputation as a good sailor. More importantly, it is light and can be transported on a car's luggage rack. The Texas 200 is not a race, and has been described as more of "a moveable messabout" from Port Isabel, Texas, near the U.S. – Mexico border, to Corpus Christi, approximately 130 miles to the north. A successful start is when the participants all head the same way, the same day.

On the third day of the cruise, when he was crossing Corpus Christi Bay in the small Cartopper, Mike turtled and was dismasted. Luckily, he was near Carl Haddick, who helped him reach the lee shore where the Puddle Duck Racer fleet of four boats were picnicking. One of the PDR skippers was Andrew Linn, who would later play a part in the Scamp story. The Puddle Duck Racers pooled their resources, truncated a donated mast with an ax, and helped Mike get on his way. Dropping out would have been understandable, but he finished with the other boats.

His next boat was a Laguna 23 that he finished in time for the 2010 Everglades Challenge. Andrew Linn crewed, and they slogged through the difficult race, finishing in five days, seventeen hours. Mike likes to think of *Laguna Dos: Blue Laguna* as his Sea Pearl beater and sailed it a lot before Jackie turned it into a flower planter.

Dylan Winter of "Keep Turning Left" fame in England once described Mike Monies as a "promiscuous boat builder." Mike laughs and agrees. He likes small craft because they allow him to be spontaneous and get on the water quickly. He acknowledges that financial considerations play a part, but ease of rigging and low maintenance are also prime considerations.

When John Welsford, and an old friend of Mike and Jackie's, emailed them a sketch of the Scamp, Mike knew he had to build one. Consequently, he was primed for a new project when Andrew Linn called and asked Mike if he was going to do the Everglades Challenge in March, 2011. Mike responded in the affirmative, and said he was going to do it solo in *Small Craft Advisor*'s newly designed Scamp. Andrew picks up the story in Small Craft Advisor (issue #70):

Too diplomatic to tell Mike he is nuts to try and sail the Everglades Challenge solo, I offered an alternative—an alternative so impossible I was sure he'd turn it down. I said, 'Tell you what, Mike, you build two Scamps—you sail one, and I'll sail the other. We'll do the Everglades Challenge as a team.' Ha! There was no way Mike would accept this offer: the Scamp design had not been finalized yet and there simply wouldn't be time to build the boats. I was so sly—I'd offered to help with no real risk of being taken up on it.

I should have known better. Mike readily agreed—and almost immediately Small Craft Advisor pledged to provide the plans free of charge and sponsor us in the event—including the $350 entry fee for each of us.

The Scamp had gone public and the first two plans-built boat were in the works. The plans for the ten-foot four-inch long Scamp arrived, and Mike set to work attempting to build two boats in one hundred days. Originally, Mike wanted to name the first plans-built Scamp the *John W.* after John Welsford, whom Mike considers a design genius. There are many skippers who agree with that assessment, but as he was building two boats, Mike decided to name the hull that he would sail the *Red Scamp*, and Andrew's boat the *Blue Scamp.*

Josh immediately called from Port Townsend. "Stop!" The Scamp had just grown. Undeterred, Mike pressed ahead with the larger design, more determined than ever to finish the two boats. He also refined and modified the Scamp, documented in *Small Craft Advisor* (issue #70):

I made a few changes to my two Scamps to improve comfort and handling for the Everglades Challenge and beyond. None of these changes affect the basic design of this wonderful little boat, but they do make it more comfortable and easier to use. One addition, the stern boarding ladder, is also a major safety addition.

Mike also widened the seats, modified the rowing seat, changed the hatch covers, and modified the skegs on the bottom. He made a major change to the mast raising system and cut a slot in the cabin top so he could easily walk the mast up from the cockpit. From the first, it was a race—could he finish the two boats in time? He almost made it. The Red Scamp was ready, but the Blue Scamp was only three-fourths complete. A lone Scamp would debut at the Everglades Challenge. Mike continues the story:

The Everglades Challenge is advertised as a 300-mile adventure that starts at Fort De Soto Park, thirteen miles southwest of St. Petersburg, and runs south down the western coast of Florida to round Cape Sable, and then eastward across Florida Bay to finish at Key Largo. It is staged by the Watertribe, and every year lures a collection of approximately seventy small boats ranging from kayaks and canoes to multihulls.

Photo: unknown

The Red Scamp
Mike Monies and friend

It is not unusual for over half of the starters to drop out as they progress from checkpoint to checkpoint. It is an endurance test every mile of the way, and for Mike and Andrew, the ultimate test would come in Florida Bay, on the southern tip of the Everglades. Mike sets the scene with a sure eye that demonstrates a keen awareness of place:

Florida Bay is best thought of as a slightly wetter extension of the Everglades between the southern most land part of the glades and the Florida Keys. It has mangrove keys, which do not have any real land under them, and vast flats of turtle grass. The grass flats have a very soft mud bottom. Try to walk and you sink way above your knees into the soft quick sand-like mud. This mud, when disturbed, gives off a very strong rotten egg order. Despite the soft mud bottom, the water over the grass is crystal clear. Most of Florida Bay is within the bounds of Everglades National Park and is highly protected. Air Boats and personal watercraft are not allowed, and power boats must stay in marked channels except for a few deep holes. The fines for disturbing the grass flats are very large, $5,000 is common, and they can go way up from there.

Florida in general, and the Everglades in particular, have been in drought conditions. Water levels over the past several years have gone way down. This has rendered many maps of the area, including the Top Spot map we were using, out of date. The newer maps such as the one sold at the Flamingo marina solve this problem by simply not showing specific depths, and using different colors to show shallow and less shallow areas. They might as well just say "Abandon all hope ye who enter here."

Access to Florida Bay is very limited. From the north, the Flamingo visitor center and marina is hard to reach, and there is only one forty-mile access road from Florida City. There are tour boats out of Flamingo for the freshwater and saltwater areas, and fishing guides work out of the marina. There is also access from the Florida Keys by boat. The main tourist attraction is the bird life with migrating birds as well as local ones numbering in the hundreds of species. It is into this environment that the Everglades Challenge comes each year.

The start of the March 2011 Everglades Challenge was captured on YouTube and shows a pack of kayaks, trimarans, catamarans, and a few exotic monohulls launching into a brisk wind. Near the end of the four-minute video, in the background, a small red-hulled boat with a white polytarp sail rests quietly and unassumingly on the sand waiting to launch.

The Red Scamp, crewed by Mike and Andrew was ready to go. The camera pans the departure, and again, you can catch a glimpse of the Scamp as Mike and Andrew get under way. An astute observer will note that it is sailing upright and not healed over. Andrew tells the first half of the story in *Small Craft Advisor* (issue # 70):

My first view of the Scamp was as it sat on a trailer in the parking lot of a La Quinta in St. Petersburg, a scant thirty-six hours before the race. It had never touched water before – heck, it'd never been rigged! The boat was so fresh the paint was barely dry. Mike and I set to work even before I put my bags in the hotel room. We worked until dark – lashing the sail to the yard and boom, attaching the jiffy reefing, figuring out the running rigging, and attaching the myriad 'fiddy parts' that make a hull a boat.

Then we got up in the morning and started working again. We splashed her at a ramp near the start of the Everglades Challenge, tested her out a little in winds in the mid-teens, hauled her out, set her on the beach at the launch site – ready to roll her down to the water when the race started at dawn the next day.

At dawn, there was a collective 'Whoop!' as seventy-one boats were pushed into the surf; forty kayaks and canoes, twelve monohulls, and nineteen multihulls hit the water and took off in 10-15 mph, south-southeast winds. This was a tough Everglades Challenge from the beginning with several boats encountering difficulties even before they got out of Tampa Bay. The waves were a little over two feet and came at intervals of less than three seconds – really a nasty chop – and the wind directly in our teeth, doing its best to confound any forward progress.

At just twelve feet long, a Scamp is no speedster, but it's no slouch either. We often hit speeds of over 6 mph, but most of the time we were struggling along at less than half that as we pinched the wind, trying to get as much velocity made good as we could. We struggled all day and all night, and most of the next day, fighting our way to Checkpoint One in conditions that ranged from windy with chop to no wind but still a nasty chop. By the time we arrived, I was frustrated, angry, sullen, and more than a little scared of what was to come. One of my friends and fellow competitors, Scott Widmire, summed it up nicely: 'It just wasn't fun anymore.'

Scott and eleven other boats dropped out at Checkpoint One: six kayaks/canoes, two monohulls, and four multihulls. Of the seventy-one boats that took to the water, only fifty-nine were continuing.

The passage to Checkpoint Two was even worse. We headed out as evening fell and ran all night under double reefs. I ran us aground in Pine Island Sound and had a bad moment rowing against the tide at Indian Pass near Checkpoint Two, where we signed the logbook at 2:30 a.m., roughly thirty-three hours after leaving Checkpoint One. I really wanted to drop out and I think Mike might have been considering it, but when the sun came up we got moving and started the run to Checkpoint Three.

Another fifteen boats dropped out at Checkpoint Two: six kayaks/canoes, four monohulls, and five multihulls; those who had been seventy-one were now forty-four.

The leg to Checkpoint Three at Flamingo was the worst yet. Thunderstorms were threatening; we got caught in one squall with winds approaching thirty mph, and the wind and waves were against us every inch of the way. We made a trifling eleven miles in eight hours, and sometime in the darkest part of the night, came close to capsizing right after we'd put in the second reef. I'm not sure a Scamp can be capsized – we only took on a quart or two of water – but I was shaken. I wanted this trip to end and end now. I even contemplated cutting the halyard – forcing us to call the Coast Guard for an extraction. Instead I just gave up, forced Mike to do all the sailing, and curled up on the seat, waiting for this nightmare to be over.

People say 'Things look different in the light of day,' but I'm here to tell you that's not true. When the sun came up, things, looked worse. The wind was really blowing stink now: twenty mph and right in our teeth. It took us over a dozen tacks to round Cape Sable and enter Florida Bay – and after all that effort, conditions just got worse. We had been under the lee of the land, but were now subject to the full force of the wind. Our two-foot chop became a three-foot chop, with a healthy sprinkling of four-foot rogues for fun. Checkpoint Three – Flamingo, with a store and restaurant – was right there! I could see the radio tower, and it was still to windward. All day we fought our way to the harbor at Flamingo, finally arriving about 3:30 p.m. on Wednesday. Jackie, Mike's wife, was there to greet us, but she'd missed our entrance. Both Mike and I just stared blankly at her when she said, 'Go back and come in again – I want to get some pictures.'

Another eleven boats dropped out at Checkpoint Three: ten kayak/canoes and one multihull. With only thirty-three competitors left, in the race, we were down to less than half.

We left Flamingo the next evening. We'd waited for the winds to come around from the north, as predicted by the robot on the NOAA radio. We dropped a hook off a small island and waited for daylight so we could navigate the narrow channels on the quickest route to the finish at Key Largo. I was feeling pretty good at this point; we had a piddling thirty-six miles to go. The sunset was a fiery red, and for the first time in days, I was delighted.

Dawn couldn't come quick enough. We set off at the first hint of daylight. We were searching for a spot where three channels branch off – northeast, east, and southeast – we wanted east. Expecting channel markers, we scanned the seas for any markers at all. We thought we saw markers to the south, and quickly ran into shallow water. My GPS showed we were near a channel, so we kept heading south until we were in it. What we though thad been channel markers were actually wading birds. We'd been led into the southeast channel by mistake.

I had the charts out and could see where we wanted to be – about three miles eastward. If we shot straight across we'd be fine. The charts showed at least a foot of depth, so we took off, confident we'd be eating fried conch by afternoon. Suddenly, we were shoaling: I could see the tops of sea grass in the water below us, then fields of sea grass, then we were aground.

I tried getting out of the boat, but my leg sank thigh-deep in the mud without meeting resistance. I had to do something. I needed something like snowshoes, so I tied seat cushions to my feet and hopped out. With me pushing and Mike working the sails, we were able to drive ourselves further into the shallows. I hit the oars and was able to force our way even further, until we were a good 700 yards from where we first ran aground.

As I tried to catch my breath after my exertions, Mike surveyed our surroundings: the water had dropped so much that seagrass we had been sailing over was now floating on top of the water. We had a depth of about four inches. No matter – it was just low tide, right? Sort of. The north wind that should have driven us right to Key Largo was also blowing all the water out of Florida Bay. The tide went out from underneath us, and it didn't come back.

We were well and truly stuck. I was the heaviest thing in the boat, and if I got out, Mike still couldn't get her to move by working the sails – and I couldn't really "get out" anyway – the mud was deep and soft. The best I could do was tie the fenders to my feet so I'd only sink up to my knees. I couldn't "walk" more than a few feet before the mud sucked the fenders sideways or frontways or backways and I had to get back into the boat and retie them. The island was of no use; every inch was covered with impenetrable mangrove. Our only option was to wait for more water, either from the tide or a shift in the wind.

We spent the first night relaxing and looking at the charts, optimistic that we would get some water under our keel and be able to get out. If we could just get around this mangrove-covered island to the east, we'd be in deeper water. We put our plan to work in the morning: through my jumping out and pushing and Mike's working the sail, we were able to get to the other side, where we drove the boat into the mud again.

With no tide coming and the wind not shifting, I phoned the park rangers at Flamingo to find out our options. They said they'd send out a boat to take a look and determine a course of action. Right after I spoke to them, a guide fisherman plowed his high-powered boat into the shallows next to the island. We called out, asking if he could tow us. He said no, but he could take us out if needed. 'No thanks,' we replied, 'the rangers will be along any minute. They'll get us out.' The fishing guide and his clients took off and we waited for the rangers to save us. A couple of hours later, I noticed some activity; a boat had pulled up about two miles to the east. It was the rangers, looking at us through binoculars. They called us and told us there was nothing they could do – we were smack dad in the middle of a huge 'sensitive area' and they could not get any closer to us. If we had a medical emergency, they'd be happy to call the Coast Guard to have us helicoptered out, but we'd have to leave all our gear and the boat would be declared abandoned.

We had plenty of food and water and were relatively comfortable (Scamp is a very roomy boat) so we thought we'd wait and see what Jackie could come up with back at Flamingo. She was working furiously behind the scenes in our behalf.

A Boat Called Scamp

We considered and discarded dozens of plans, from unloading all unessential gear and one crew member (me) to see it the boat would sail (she would not) to setting the boat on fire so at least no one would profit from our abandoning it. (OK, I admit those were both my plans, as were many others, several even more outlandish.) In the end, we decided our best course of action would be to wrestle the boat back to the west side of the island. Marginally closer to where we might find deep water. Once again, it was fenders to my feet and over the side, only this time I tuckered myself out so much I almost didn't make it back into the boat. If Mike hadn't grabbed my life jacket, I'd still be standing in the mud.

The sun went down, the sun came up – our third night on the Scamp. Dawn found us just as stuck, just as helpless. Jackie called and told us she had a plan: an extraction by canoe and kayak, We just needed to wait.

So here I am, the afternoon wearing on, and as comfortable as the Scamp is, I'm getting tired of Florida Bay. For the hundredth time, I scan the horizon, looking for any sign of activity. I can see the ranger boat off in the distance – the same place they observed us from yesterday. By straining my eyes, I can just make out some movement. "Mike, can I borrow your binoculars for a second?"

Yep, there's a kayak and a canoe approaching. It's beginning to look like I won't be spending the rest of my life in the mud after all.

Esther Luft and Wayne Albert, owners and operators of the Paddle House, are slowly making their way towards us. Wayne is using a kayak paddle to propel the canoe something I find vaguely offensive but acceptable, under the circumstances. When they arrive we hold a brief conference. The options are few: the tides will not come back for a week or more, until the next full moon, at least. Our plan has always been for me to leave the boat, taking as much gear as practical, lightening the boat as much as possible, but we knew the boat wouldn't float enough to sail. 'The rangers said they won't declare your boat derelict if you secure an anchor to it,' Esther says. 'You can come get it when the water comes back in the bay.'

That seals it for me, but Mike needs a little more convincing. In the end, we all leave together. Wayne in the front of the canoe, Mike in the middle, me at the back. The canoe is overloaded and we are scraping bottom the entire two miles to the ranger boat. This paddle is the most physically demanding thing I have done in a long time. Wayne appears to be more of a machine than a man, and I can only try and keep up. Shoulders aching, back breaking, we finally arrive and this damnable adventure can enter its final phase.

Besides us, two other boats couldn't make it from Checkpoint Three to the finish; a kayak and a multihull. Of the 71 original starters, only 30 (just 42%) boats finished and earned the coveted shark's tooth necklace.

I'm pretty sure this has been my last Everglades Challenge, and in truth, I have taken to humming a song from the movie Toy Story – Randy Newman's "I'll Go Sailing No More."

The 2011 Everglades Challenge had not ended well for the Red Scamp and its two intrepid crew; however, Mike and Andrew's goal had never been to win the race, but rather to prove the Scamp's mettle as a microcruiser. Mike critically evaluated the Scamp in the same issue of Small Craft Advisor:

Andrew and I agree that the well-designed Scamp can take a lot more than her crew. She is an awesome little cruiser.

With her centerboard and rudder down she tacks quickly and flawlessly in both light and heavy air. Just put the rudder down and she spins in little more than a boat length. The tacking angle depends on the wind and wave conditions. In moderate wind with small waves she will tack through ninety degrees. I knew that we couldn't hand-hold the sheet for 300 miles so I mounted a swivel-based fairlead and cam cleat on the port side. This made the port tack closer to the wind than the starboard tack. I will change this to get the sheet more to the center of the boat.

She does well going downwind. Only once in a very high wind did she start to death roll. This was fixed by putting in one and then both reefs which brought her back under control with no loss of speed.

In places like Florida Bay where we could not put the centerboard or rudder down all the way, we still made progress to windward. With the centerboard only down about four inches, and the rudder halfway down, she'll still tack to windward through 120 degrees. At one point when I was alone in Florida Bay, I was able to make progress to windward in less than one foot of water with the centerboard all the way up and the rudder tied up with the uphaul so it stuck straight out behind the boat. I could not tack with rudder alone but had to use the lee side oar to bring the nose into the wind. The fact that I could go to windward at all I think is due to the two skegs on bottom.

Scamp handles waves very well. She floats like a cork. I have sailed in many areas known for steep, close together waves but I have never seen anything like the random lumps of water we encountered in far south Florida – three-foot waves with very steep sides and just enough space between for Scamp to fit. Still, the only time we took on any more spray was when a random wave hit us on the side. The bow transom is high enough so it only hits one wave in a hundred, and even that doesn't slow the boat. The hobbyhorse action does not seem to take the wind out of the sails and slow progress to windward.

All in all, Scamp took very good care of us in some very tough conditions that sent other, mostly larger sailboats home.

For the Scamp, the 2011 Everglades Challenge was the ultimate shakedown cruise, and, without doubt, Mike and Andrew had proven the small craft's worth. But it was still stuck in the mud, anchored in the shallows of Florida Bay. The grounding and subsequent rescue of the Scamp is a cautionary tale for any small craft skipper contemplating sailing in the area, and the rescue reinforces the value of a great support crew. After arriving back at Flamingo with Andrew, Mike picks up the rescue of the Scamp in his own words:

Jackie and her mom were waiting for us a Flamingo. We helped Esther Luft and Wayne Albert, the owners and operators of the Paddle House, load their gear and thanked them as best we could. I gave the rangers my contact information so we could keep in touch about water conditions in the Bay. They felt it would be at least a week before I could get back to the Scamp. Tired and dirty after our three days and nights on Florida Bay, we were ready for a Florida City motel room with a hot shower and a soft bed.

The next day we all drove to Tampa to get Andrew to the airport and pick up the van we had left there. Since the start of the Everglades Challenge, Jackie and her mom had been following us with the pickup and trailer. Jackie had left the trailer at the finish in Key Largo so I wanted to get it to Flamingo. We started back south in both cars and made it to Ft. Meyers before Jackie gave out. She had worked hard to organize our extraction, and now she was having a Lupus attack. She and her mom stayed in Ft. Meyers to rest and I headed south. I finally hooked up the trailer and drove to Flamingo.

A Boat Called Scamp

It was now Wednesday and the rangers told me that with a predicted wind shift, and some tide action caused by the upcoming full moon, Saturday was my best bet for getting the Scamp out. I decided to try to get to the Scamp on Friday afternoon. I knew that Esther and Wayne would not be available so I set out to find a fishing guide. I found one who had a flats boat with a pole and poling platform, and he agreed to take me out Friday afternoon after his charter. I was waiting at the marina when he returned with has clients and after telling the rangers what we were doing, we set out for Curlew Key, and, I hoped, Scamp.

From the channel in Tin Can Pass, I saw Scamp but could not tell if she was where we had left her. The guide said he had not fished Curlew Key in several years but at one time a small channel lead off to the South to Curlew Key. We found a channel but the water soon turned shallow.

We had to stop the motor and lift it up. I was excited because there was one-foot of water over the grass where there had been just four-inches when we came out by canoe. If I could get to Scamp, she would be afloat and moveable. But we were approaching the Key from the northeast, and as Scamp had been left near the southwest corner, I could not see her. With a strong east wind at our backs poling the boat was easy.

We were about a quarter mile from the key when the guide decided he was going to have a very hard time poling back against the wind. He did not want to go any further downwind for fear he could not pole back before dark. I could get out here and crawl the rest of the way or go back to Flamingo with him. I paid him and went over the side. With my PFD, I was floating enough to crawl using my hands and feet. The guide turned his boat around and started poling into the wind. I still could not see Scamp and could only hope it was still there. I crawled the one-fourth mile to the Key and looked back. The guide had made it back to Tin Can Pass, and had his motor running again. I still could not see

Scamp, but as I crawled around the end of the Key she was there, just another 150 yards to go.

I washed as much mud off as I could on the boarding ladder. Back on board, I found everything just as we had left it. A quick call to Jackie to let her know Scamp and I were ok, and I made ready to set sail. It was getting dark fast but that big full moon was up and I could see enough to sail. My goal was Buoy Key and Tin Can Channel, directly into the wind. I started tacking upwind with no centerboard and the rudder in the up position. Thanks to the two skegs, Scamp made progress to windward but I had to use the lee oar to turn the bow through the wind when tacking. The moon was so bright Scamp cast a shadow but I could no longer see the bottom. We got stuck again in the grass near the southeast corner of Buoy key, just one hundred yards from the channel. My clothes were still wet so I took them off and got into a sleeping bag for my fourth night on Florida Bay.

Saturday morning I woke to the sound of powerboats in the channel. I could see that I was stuck on a high spot just 50 feet from one-foot deep water that seemed to join with Tin Can channel on the north end of the Key. I tried to get out and push but the boat would not move. I got back in to wait for the expected high tide. The ranger boat that had helped with our extraction the previous Sunday came down the channel, and I gave them the thumbs up to let them know I was ok. I stuck a stick in the mud with a mark showing the current water line and waited.

By 1:00 PM, the water had come up three-eights of an inch. By 1:30 it was up one inch and I decided to go for it. This time when I got out of the boat I could just move it. The wind was still very strong out of the East making Buoy Key a lee shore all the way to the channel. I finally reached water one-foot deep less than twenty feet from the floating mat of dead grass that passes for a shoreline around these keys. If I had let the boat get blown into that mess, it would be very hard to remove.

A Boat Called Scamp

Once Scamp was floating, the strong wind almost ripped the boat out of my grasp. I held on tight to the aft port quarter and started moving north. In one-foot deep water, I could walk the boat forward but I was sinking up to my knees with each step. In a few spots where the water was less than one-foot deep, I had to crawl on my knees. It took over thirty minutes of hard work to reach the north end of Buoy Key where the channel touches the Key. Still in the water, I reached into the boat, grabbed the anchor, and set it. Again, I washed the mud off at the boarding ladder and climbed aboard.

My plan was to catch my breath, get a drink of water, let the rudder down and set a double-reef for a downwind sail to Flamingo. No sooner had I grabbed my water bottle than the anchor started dragging. I was heading right for the end of Buoy Key and a fixed channel marker. A few frantic strokes on the port side oar got me into the channel, just missing the marker. The Scamp was being blown downwind, the way I wanted, dragging the anchor with the rudder up. I got the anchor aboard and let down the rudder. Now I could turn around and see what was happening. The channel that I had been trying to get to for over a week was only about thirty-feet wide, and not deep enough to let the rudder all the way down. I was being blown downwind at about four mph with no sail. The channel went downwind for as far as I could see and I had enough steerage to keep the boat in the channel. It seemed like a good idea to just keep going under bare poles.

The ranger boat that I had seen in the morning going east was coming up behind me, now going west. They were at idle speed because this area was too shallow for even their fancy boat to get up on a plane. It took them a long time to pass me and they were surprised at how fast I was going with no sail up.

I was able to keep in the channel all the way to the south end of Joe Kemp Key, the very area where Andrew and I had made our fateful mistake. I put up some sail to tack the last quarter mile up the Flamingo channel and into the marina. This took 45 minutes of short tacking to windward. I finally made the entrance to the marina and took down my sail. I rowed up to the dock by the boat ramp where the rangers were there to help me tie up. We were all glad this ordeal was finally over. The rangers told me they had gone all the way to Crocodile Dragover on their patrol today and that there was almost no water there. That area had been on our original course to Key Largo. They said next time to plan on going the long way around. I loaded the boat on its trailer for the trip to a Motel and a hot meal.

Many friends and the folks who had been following our adventure created a 'Save the Scamp' fund through Duckworks, and their generosity allowed us to stay in Florida the ten days it took to get Scamp home. We can never thank them, Esther, Wayne, and those great rangers enough.

Will there be a next time? Well, I have learned to never say "Never."

There is an afterword to Mike and Andrew's adventure. A discerning skipper will probably be asking what happened to those fines that Mike had mentioned for disturbing the grass flats. Jackie Monies credits Esther Luft of the Paddle House for pleading their case to the rangers. By a mix of charm and understanding, she explained the situation to the rangers in the way they understood. As a result, relations were improved all around.

For Mike and Andrew, time will put their adventure in perspective. But make no mistake, the Everglades Challenge had tested them beyond all expectations, and a sturdy little red boat is still sailing.

Enter Gig Harbor BoatWorks

From the very first, Josh and Craig knew that a commercially-built fiberglass version of the Scamp was critical if it was to be anything other than a cult boat with a small but fanatical following. As mentioned above, the vast majority of small craft skippers are not builders and simply want to be on the water with a minimum of fuss and effort. But turning the wooden design into fiberglass reality was no small task, and would take engineering skill combined with a love of small boats and an exceeding amount of patience. Fortunately, Josh had just the man in mind, Dave Robertson, the founder, owner, and proprietor of Gig Harbor BoatWorks, located seventy miles away in Gig Harbor, Washington.

Dave Robertson is the type of engineer who inspires confidence and trust. He's in his mid sixties, pleasant in appearance, with gray hair and eyes. He describes himself as "A stage-three engineer" whose motto is "Versatility and Simplicity." The sixteen-foot Melonseed Gig Harbor Boat Works makes is a perfect example of his philosophy. The graceful boat can be rowed, sailed, or motored, and is amazingly fast.

Dave built his first boat, a hydroplane, when he was thirteen, and it was only natural when he started to build boats in the 1970s. He was doing his engineering thing in the late '70s and needed a tender for his Mercator 30 sailboat. As there was nothing that met his needs, he decided to build his own and Gig Harbor Boat Works was born. What was meant as a hobby took off, and he retired from managing a steel mill, with four days off a month, to concentrate on building small boats.

The rest, as they say, is history, and he currently produces about 100 boats a year.

The boat works moved to its current location in 1987, which is a short drive up Peacock Avenue in Gig Harbor. The tree-lined road rises rapidly with the harbor at your back, and one cannot help but think it is great place to build boats. Near the top of the hill, a modest sign announces Gig Harbor Boat Works and a right turn leads down a narrow lane behind a house flying the American flag.

The small boat shop is in the middle of a grassy meadow with a few covered boats stored out front awaiting shipment. The shop itself is a two-bay affair with room for a small office. It is essentially a three-man organization with Dave, Falk Bock, and Dave Gahan. Dave describes Falk as his "right arm," and Dave Gahan is his fiberglass and finishing department.

Josh first approached Dave early in 2011 about producing the boat. Dave liked what he saw and knew it would fit in with Gig Harbor's production and not compete with the other boats in the line. The Scamp was easy to row, sail, or motor, was fast for its size, and met Dave's design philosophy of "Versatility and Simplicity." As he would soon learn, that did not mean the Scamp would be a simple boat to produce in fiberglass. And it would not be cheap.

Dave's eyes light up when he discusses the process, and he describes it as, "Not really an engineering project, but an art project." But he is a businessman and also speaks of "trajectories" and "expanding markets," and creating the molds for a new boat is an expensive process.

He needed to test the market before committing, and put out the word in the small craft community that he was accepting deposits. He needed six buyers before starting production. It would take a lot of patience on the part of the skippers so Dave sweeten the deal with a low introductory price of $12,750 which included the rigging, sail, and trailer.

Josh told this author that Gig Harbor was accepting deposits and ten minutes later, on Wednesday, July 27, 2011, Dave had the first order. But it would take some time for the next five orders to trickle in, and there was a boatload of design, planning, and scheduling to work through.

Gig Harbor took the plunge and started work on the plug for the hull mold in the summer of 2012. From the start, Dave solicited input from everyone who had dealt with the Scamp. The constraints of mold-making dictated much of what he could do, but also offered other opportunities. He was determined to refine the design and incorporate changes that would make it a better boat. When faced with an engineering problem is given to "napkin doodling" until he gets it right. Two examples are the "Scamp ramp" he built into the cabin top that made it easier to lift the mast into place, and extending the gunwales back to the transom.

It would take another year before hull number one rolled out of the shop.

The Testing of the *B. Frank*

It was the Spring of 2012, and to quote the opening lines of Chaucer's Canterbury Tales, "Thanne longen folk to goon on pilgrimages." Dan Phy was no exception, and he was soon hooking up the *B. Frank*, the first kit-built Scamp, and trailering eastward from the Pacific Coast to the balmy climes of northern Florida. Once in Florida, the *B. Frank* was adopted by Steve Haines, which is a story best left untold.

While Howard Rice had wrung the boat out and put it through capsize tests, and Mike Monies had subjected it to the hell of the Everglades Challenge, there was still much to learn about the boat. The little craft does not always inspire confidence at first glance, and, as one old skipper observed, "It's just too cute." It was time to test the Scamp in a different environment, without a dedicated support team, over a longer time frame, and away from the amenities of civilization. Steve Haines had the perfect proving ground for the *B. Frank*—the Apalachicola River. A launch date of Wednesday, April 11, 2012, looked very promising.

Steve is an active conservationist and a graduate of the Florida Master Naturalist Program. He believes in doing and helps to clean up bayous, replant sea grass, and sow scallops. He was taken with the beauty of the Apalachicola when he went on a night cruise twenty-five years ago, and has wanted to go back ever since. It is lush and isolated river, and while there are signs of man's work, it remains undeveloped, almost primitive. The philosopher in Steve wonders what the Spanish explorers saw five centuries ago.

The route Steve proposed to sail down the Apalachicola extended 105 miles from Chattahoochee to Apalachicola Bay on the Gulf of Mexico. He assured Dan that the Scamp was perfect of the voyage with its short mast and shallow draft. Steve told the story of "Down the Lazy River" in issue #78 of Small Craft Advisor:

76

The river murmured under stars and a half moon, and I dozed under Scamp's veranda, while Dan slept on the sand bar a hundred feet away. The air was cool and quiet, except for rustling leaves and creaking branches. There was some soft bird talk, and the mullet never slept. This was a perfect place, and I was in it, having found that narrow zone between resting and waking. A silent observer, I took in this river music as though I was not too near, not too far away.

Photo: Dan Phy

Getting Serious
Steve Haines and Dan Phy enroute to the Apalachicola

There was a splash, then another, then a footstep in the water, very near, and my eyes opened wide as my pulse quickened. Another footstep, and I sat up, listening. Another halting step, just off the starboard side now, and I moved there quietly. Pausing for my eyes to catch up, I snatched the boom tent back as a white heron squawked, splashed, and took flight. I exhaled a short word and relaxed, shining my light around. The water was full of minnows, drawn to the eddy created by Scamp, and the big bird had come to dine. Sorry, buddy.

The beginnings of this river are in north Georgia. It wanders through fields and towns, is bridged and delayed by dam formed lakes, but it pushes on, joined by other streams, and makes its way to the Gulf of Mexico. It was home to the Apalachee people, now long gone, then to the Spanish, English, and to us.

The Apalachicola River as such starts at Chattahoochee, just below the dam, which forms Lake Seminole. It was on the southeast bank, at River Landing Park, that we would launch. But the planning had started long before, and the trip actually began when Dan Phy left Ft. Bragg, California, with the B. Frank in tow.

The idea was to see this lightly populated area over a period of a few days, overnighting on sandbars, sailing as much as possible, motoring when we must. Gear was selected for practicality, durability, and minimum impact. Provisions were simple, but more than adequate, as we were aware that resupply would be difficult once we pushed off.

On launch day, we left Panama City, and, after a side trip to Two Egg, were at the river's edge. In less than an hour, we were afloat, with gear aboard and stowed and the sail up. Final plans were made for departure, check-ins with home, and arrival in Apalachicola, 105.5 miles down the sailing line. Winds were forecast at 10-12 from the north, though it didn't feel like it down on the river. But the temperature was in the high 70's and the sky clear.

A young local fellow had seen and admired Scamp, and was surprised to learn of our plans. He told us that alligators up to thirty feet ply this river, and that we should watch out for them, which we promised to do.

Pam, my wife, stood ready to take pictures from the floating dock as we shoved B. Frank's nose upstream with the helm over. The current turned us downstream, and we were underway. The sail filled, and we ran quickly, with Pam scrambling to get pictures before we were out of range. The GPS quickly passed 5mph, then 6, and stayed around 6.5. The wind was not strong, the river nearly flat, and the sailing effortless, with B. Frank touching 6.9 several times. It was pretty clear that Scamp pays little attention to hull speed, which piques the curiosity as to her potential.

I had been aboard Scamp 1 at Port Townsend for a few minutes, with Howard Rice at the helm. But this was my first time at the helm, and a day I will not forget. Perfect weather, beautiful scenery, comfortable cockpit, responsive helm, and a good turn of speed are hard to beat.

We saw our first alligator, and then another. They didn't look to be thirty feet, but they were intimidating, even at a distance. One came off the bank with a big splash, then paced us for a minute before turning toward the bank.

In less than an hour we passed far below the Interstate 10 bridge, and soon we looked up to see Gregory House, a mansion perched high above the river at Torreya State Park, on the east bank. We had considered making this our first stop, but we were there early, and it was not a good place to go ashore, so we pressed on.

We had seen several sandbars, and any might have made a good place to stop. Almost every place else, trees came to the water's edge, and fallen trees and branches were common hazards, but easily spotted and avoided. There were several sets of rock dikes, built for erosion control, which ran at right angles to the riverbank, jutting to the edge of the channel. Some had snags stuck on them, intruding into the channel, making the middle of the river the best place to be.

As the banks rose, the wind was often blocked, and changed direction and strength often. Still, Scamp was perfectly controllable, as long as there was wind, and I managed to avoid hitting anything, except for a large submerged post, which I saw right after the centerboard bounced off of it. There were times when the wind carried us away from the eddy currents, and times when it put us into them. Other times, the current tried to take us one way, the wind another, when we needed to go someplace else altogether. Sailing under these conditions was quite different from lake or bay sailing, and Dan's river kayaking experience was invaluable in helping read the river.

From time to time, the current overcame the helm, resulting in an upstream turn; sometimes we were carried sideways or backwards, but we always avoided the obstacles. Eventually, I came to use this counterintuitive tactic deliberately, and labeled it the "B. Frank Maneuver." It worked, and we didn't hit anything.

It is important to be ashore well before dark, and by 6 pm we had found a nice spot just downstream from one of the rock dikes, on the east bank. A small sandbar provided a great place for our first night, and Scamp's nose was on the sand. Just under the sand, though, was sticky mud, which was hard to wash off. This was the only place we found that mud on the trip, but we watched for it.

A Boat Called Scamp

A mushroom anchor, chain, and rode were stored in a five-gallon plastic bucket on the port side of the veranda, and the sand made burying the anchor easy. Tracks showed that wild hogs, deer, and raccoons were regular visitors here, and a large area near the woods had been rooted by the hogs.

Twigs and sticks from the sandbar provided plenty of fuel for the Kelly Kettle, and the coffee was soon ready. Dan's one-man backpacking tent went up, along with Scamp's simple ripstop boom tent, and our first night's camp was ready, over 17 miles downstream.

By 7:15, the sun was below the west bank, and by 8:00, it was very dark. The sounds of insects and birds changed against the rivers, and the air cooled quickly into the high 40's. But Scamp's cockpit and tent, along with an air mattress and lightweight sleeping bag, were level, dry, and comfortable.Heavy dew underscored the importance of the boom tent, and every night on the river was wet, even without rain. Our wood was wet, too, but we still managed to get the kettle going. After that, though, we started keeping our dry wood overnight in a plastic bag. Before leaving, we made sure we had left nothing behind, and buried the few ashes left by the Kelly Kettle.

We took our time getting under way, but soon worked our way past Blountstown and Bristol, where the wind made sailing under the bridge challenging. There were a few fishermen out, and all waved and stayed well clear. Ahead, a pair of fishermen pulled along the bank, and had just stopped when they boated a fish at least three feet long.

Here and there were floating houses, tied to big trees. Many were small and simple, but some were newer, and appeared well appointed. Most can only be reached by boat, and locals have been using them for generations for getaways. Some appeared to have full time liveaboards, though.

A pair of young guys in a small fishing boat passed us going downstream, and we met them an hour or so later as they came back toward us. Well ahead, they throttled back and idled toward us, leaving no wake. They were curious about Scamp and our trip, and followed along behind, starting the motor to catch up when a breeze moved us ahead. I was impressed by their courtesy, and we wished each other well as they headed north to Bristol.

We passed bluffs of chalk and alum, and towing trees. There were times that the eddies might have taken us into the snags, but for Dan's quick use of a paddle with a folding shaft. Oars were stowed on the sole, but it was quicker to paddle, and Scamp is light and responsive enough for it to work well.

At the helm, I sat to starboard and Dan stayed forward on the port side. The aft floor compartment held our trash, including empty water bottles and well-protected Wag-Bags. The forward floor compartment kept our water reasonably cool and easy to reach. Snacks, mostly fruit, were in the shade of the veranda, or in the lockers there, along with other gear. Storage was never a problem, and we actually had plenty of room left over. We did not take a cooler or ice, though we could have.

Dan was nursing a knee injury when we started on the trip, but managed well. Climbing back aboard the boat after a stop, though, I zigged, he zagged and stepped in a hole, further injuring the knee. It was a bad thing, but we pressed on.

Our second camp was on a large sandbar without the mud we'd found upstream. Like the first site, it was covered with animal tracks, and there was considerable damage from pigs rooting by the woods. Camp and coffee were quickly made, and another night began.

It was here that the bird and I startled each other, and here that the Big Dipper looked like it was going to scoop out the trees. It was here, too, that wisps of fog stood straight and marched downstream, against flat fog-clouds going upstream. They met silently over the river, just off the transom.

After breakfast, we got started, again making sure to leave no trash or ash. It didn't occur to either of us that this was Friday the 13th. It was a difficult sailing day, though, with a rising wind that tried to stay on Scamp's nose, and a serpentine river with steep banks and plenty of snags. We found a good place to stop and knocked off early, planning to get an early start.

We left our camp above the Wewahitchka cutoff early, but the wind was already up, and the NOAA radio forecast 15-20 from the south. There were some whitecaps on the river, and we were taken aback a few times, and relied on the now tested "B. Frank Maneuver" several times to stay nearer the middle of the river. The middle course avoided snags better, but the wind was stronger, so we bowed to practicality and started the motor. The choice was easier because we weren't gaining ground, and it was getting to be frustrating work.

The Suzuki 2.5 horse 4 stroke short-shaft was quick to start, and ran perfectly. On the adjustable mount, a long shaft is not needed, and the prop didn't come out of the water, even in sporting conditions. The 1 liter tank needs some breathing room near the gas cap, though, and will tell you if you overfill it. At 1/2 to 3/4 throttle, we pushed through stiff headwinds, usually making between 5 and 6 mph. There were times when we rounded a bend and took it on the chin, slowing to as little as 3.5 for a second or two before regaining speed. This happened when the wind had so overpowered the current that channel markers were flattened out, pointing upstream. I was surprised when I calculated our fuel consumption at better than 25 miles per gallon through the water.

Photo: Dan Phy
The *B. Frank* Explaining Life to Steve Haines
"Grasshopper, sail with joy but always check your six for alligators."

Saturday morning near Wewahitchka found lots of people fishing, and lots of boats were up in the bushes, and many didn't see us. They were fishing. I have family and friends there, and wondered if any were out there. We passed apiaries, set back from the bank, where bees make honey from the tupelo blossoms, and many camp houses. There were many small creeks that joined the river, and the views were like looking up into forested tunnels. These might provide shelter in a blow, and with the mast down, Scamp would be perfect for exploring.

A Boat Called Scamp

We made good time, and might have made Apalachicola Saturday night. But it is likely that we'd have run out of daylight, and we had not seen or heard one boat out after dark since we'd been on the river.

We wanted to get to the beer and oysters around noon on Sunday, and once we were within striking distance, we started looking for sandbars. Below Ft. Gadsden, we found one on the east bank, and were quickly anchored just downstream from a camphouse.

The sand was coarser here, but there was no mud, and there were deep tracks in the sand. Behind the beach was a vast cypress swamp, and the insects were loud. Unlike our other sites, there was plenty of trash around.

About 75 yards downstream, a family played in the water. The river was wider there, and rolling against the wind, but it was still a beautiful place on a fine day. It was then that the insects, buzzed louder, or so I thought. From around the next bend, like the smokers from "Waterworld," came a pack of personal watercraft. There were eight of them, and four or five had two aboard. All but one buzzed us before beaching.

They were loud, and I winced at the thought of them partying all night on the beach. But they didn't stay, and, after rocking our boat as they blasted off, passing within 25 feet or so of our stern, they were gone. They won the prize for being the only rude people we encountered on the trip.

From down the beach, a Chevy pickup slowly made its way toward us, and stopped in the tracks when it got close. It was then that we met Danny and Coy, oystermen from Eastpoint, across the bridge from Apalachicola. They were curious about Scamp and our trip, and a trove of local knowledge. When they learned that we hadn't brought beer, they insisted that we drink some of theirs, and invited us to go into town for some entertainment. They offered to take us oystering or shrimping another time, but said it was too rough in the bay to go this weekend. They were right.

Cell service had been surprisingly good until our last stop, but Coy had told me that I might get service within a short walk of there, and he was right. I was able to call home and confirm our plans.

Next morning, we headed out into it, and slogged downstream. Our plan was to haul out at the ramp below the Gorrie Bridge. But under the conditions, we decided to head up Scipio Creek to a more sheltered area.

About five miles upstream, I thought I saw a sailboat behind us, but then wasn't sure. The conditions demanded that I watch ahead, and it was easy to crab over toward the shallows. This was not a day to go aground, even in grass, so I paid attention.

The chop was stiff, but we took very little water aboard. That happened when a wave slapped the side of the bow and came up, and the wind blew it into my face. But it was splashes, not gallons, or even pints.

We turned up Scipio Creek and waved while Pam took pictures from the deck of Up The Creek Raw Bar. There are docks just below the Bar, and, to our pleasant surprise, a ramp. Scamp was quickly alongside, and almost as quickly, we were upstairs and into some cold beer and very good food. From upstairs, we saw the boat that had followed us; it was a blue-hulled Potter 19.

We had been watched from another dock by a salty looking fellow. He and another local, who lives on a big Southern Cross, are SCA readers, and were as happy to see a Scamp in person as we were to show them.

A couple of hours later, we were back in Panama City, cleaning the boat, unpacking, and talking about Cedar Key. But this had been a special trip, in a special boat.

For Steve and Dan, there was no doubt that the Scamp was a winner, and they were safely off the water in time to hotfoot it over to Cedar Key, Florida, for the first Small Craft Skills Academy.

Small Craft Skills Academy

The goal of the Academy is to help small craft sailors become self-reliant, and few men can do this better than Howard Rice. The word spread fast when the dates of the first four Academies were announced in issue #72 of Small Craft Advisor. The first class at Cedar Key, Florida, scheduled for April 22-25, 2012, quickly sold out and three more venues were added.

Hugh Horton signed on as an instructor and Steve was to serve as the Beach Master, keeping things organized on the shore and tracking the action on the water in case a rescue was needed. Dan had enrolled with nine other skippers and the *B. Frank* was part of the eight-boat fleet that ranged from a canoe to a West Wight Potter 19.

Photo: Dan Phy
The first Small Craft Skills Academy
Howard Rice and Dana Holsclaw recovering the *B. Frank*

It was at that academy *B. Frank* capsized for real and not as a planned demonstration. But Howard and his student quickly had the boat upright and were back on board. To everyone's amazement, they sailed away, totally unfazed by their quick dip in Cedar Key. But that is what the Academy is all about.

Scamp Camp

The Scamp world was a hubbub of activity as a variety of builders worked on their boats. Simeon Baldwin had finished the build manual, but early on, everyone involved with the Scamp understood that the boat's future depended on quality builds.

A Boat Called Scamp

Pete Leenhouts, the director of the Northwest School of Wooden Boatbuilding, watched people react to the prototype at the 2011 Wooden Boat Festival and broached the idea about teaching a class on its construction. Unfortunately, his school didn't room for any new projects, so he approached Jake Beattie at the Northwest Maritime Center about using the Center's boatshop to hold a class and build ten boats under close supervision. Josh immediately got on board and knocked the price of the kits down from the normal $2300.

Names do count, and Katie Whalen at the School christened the project "Scamp Camp." It was an idea whose time had come. Howard Rice and John Welsford were involved from the very first, and offered their services to work with Scott Jones, the current director of the Maritime Center's boatshop, in teaching the class. Naturally, Simeon Baldwin was among the first to sign up as he had a kit ready to go.

On August 6, 2012, thirteen other Scampers showed up to spend the next two weeks building ten hulls. They were a diverse group: Bryant Adams from Anacortes WA; Derek Gries, Hood River, OR; Eric Hervol, Marrowstone Island WA; Charles Koch, Boulder CO; Mike McInnis, Olive Branch MS; Keith Nasman, Portland OR; Richard Rasmussen, Brookings, OR; Tom Robb, Cayuga Falls, OH; Cliff Sell, all the way from Fuerth, Germany; Dale Simonson, Burnaby, B.C.; Ethan Stall, Bainbridge Island, WA; Bob Threlkeld, Port Townsend, WA; and Karl Wirkus, from Boise, ID.

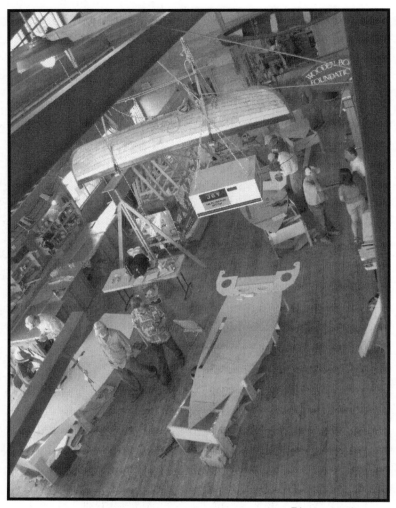

Photo: author

The First Scamp Camp
Day One—ready to go

Some would find the build challenging, others difficult, and for the experienced woodworkers, a moderate project. Throughout, Howard, John, and Scott guided the builders through the process, solving problems and refining techniques as they went.

What Kees Prins, Scott Jones, and Sarah Rudolph had started less than two years before, what Dan Phy had labored on in December of 2010, and what Mike Monies had amply proven, had now come to fruition. And more Scamp Camps were on the way.

Photo: Rob Sampson

The Key Players
(l to r) John Welsford, Howard Rice, and Josh Colvin

The Fiberglass Scamp

Meanwhile, Dave Robertson and Falk Bock were laboring in Gig Harbor, building the three plugs for the hull, interior, and deck molds. Dave was in his element solving problems by "napkin doodling," and applying plain-old engineering skills. He kept his Scampers updated with twelve progress reports, detailing the Scamp's development. Hull number one came out of the molds in the Spring of 2013 and the finishing work began in earnest.

Dave sent this author into spasms of sensory overload with the options available for his boat. High on the list were stainless steel keel guards, bronze deadlights and cleats, and mahogany gunwale trim. Finally, the boat was ready and underwent its first sea trial in July 2013. The results were outstanding and the new craft performed like a thoroughbred.

Josh Colvin had a chance to sail the craft on a second trial and photo shoot, and was very satisfied with its performance and the quality of the build.

On Friday, July 19, *Klompen*, which is Dutch for wooden shoes, was delivered to its new owner, the author of this tale. Dave Robertson and Falk Bock were justifiably proud of what they had built.

Photo: Author
Gig Harbor BoatWorks Fiberglass Hull #1
The builders: Dave Robertson (l) and Falk Bock

Klompen was promptly trailered to Port Townsend for the annual Pocket Yachter Palooza held at the Northwest Maritime Center. The Palooza is an informal gathering of small craft enthusiasts, and it was the perfect venue for the first fiberglass Scamp to make its debut in the company of four wooden Scamps.

The Palooza
The Pocket Yachters pack the Northwest Maritime Center's courtyard.

While not the bell of the ball, *Klompen* drew its fair share of interest and questions. Without doubt, the most common expression heard was "What a cute boat." Simeon Baldwin spent hours sharing his knowledge with *Klompen's* skipper and working out a few minor rigging problems, all of which were quickly resolved.

On Sunday July 21, 2013, *Klompen* was officially launched at Boat Haven Harbor in Port Townsend. Josh and Chuck Silver were there with the first Scamp along with the boatologist, Simeon Baldwin. Again, Simeon led this skipper through the art of rigging and launching a Scamp. It wasn't hard and went quickly, but the Scampers had to wait for the fog to lift.

One of the best shows in town was watching a large group of sport fishermen returning from a salmon tournament and queue up at the single dock and the narrow ramp that could only handle one boat at a time. It was an exercise in order, civility, and mutual help as the boats were quickly retrieved. This skipper's home port is in the Sacramento California area, and can assure you a similar situation at a ramp there would have required the National Guard to maintain order. But I digress.

The fog started to lift and the fishermen easily sequenced *Klompen* and *Scamp* into the process. By waiting a few minutes, *Klompen* slipped off its trailer and into the water at high noon. But there was still some work to be done. Simeon topped up the water ballast tank while *Klompen's* skipper retrieved the rudder, which had been left behind.

The two boats rowed out of the marina in calm conditions and drifted, waiting for the wind to kick up. By 1:30 they were sailing. *Klompen* sailed sweetly and performed as advertised.

The boat that Dave Robertson had refined and brought into production proved to be amazingly fast and remarkably stable. The two boats headed across the bay for Rat Island where they beached with four other boats from the Palooza. It was something to see, the very first Scamp together with the first fiberglass version.

Photo: Debra Colvin
Beached at Rat Island
(l to r) *Klompen*, Simeon Baldwin, Chuck Silver, Dick Herman, Josh Colvin, *Scamp*.

The sail back to Port Townsend later that afternoon was a thing of beauty—two Scamps zigging and zagging in sight of each other, including a pass through the shallow water "cut" between Rat and Marrowstone Islands. With the sun low in the sky, the two Scamps reached Boat Haven just as the wind died.

Klompen was quickly retrieved and examined for any dings or damage from its first formal outing. Nothing. In a way it was almost anticlimactic, but the smiles on each of our faces said it all.

Scamp was on the water.

Acknowledgements

This brief biography owes so much to so many individuals that, in all fairness, I cannot claim to be the sole author. These are the "Friends" mentioned on the title page who are also the major players in this narrative. One and all, they shared their time and experiences with this author and made this narrative possible. They are a unique group, geographically scattered over the world, but with a common touchstone – the Scamp – and I will always think of them as the original "Scampers."

I owe a special thanks to two individuals, Josh Colvin and Steve Haines. In his own quiet way, Josh is a leader and facilitator. He makes things happen. He also let me wander through the pages of his magazine and select the articles for this brief account. Steve Haines was part collaborator, part cheerleader, part editor, and always a good friend from the very start. If the gentle reader should discern a certain tongue-in-cheek voice in parts of the narrative, that's Steve's influence at work. But above all, he kept me on track.

As always, any mistakes and omissions are mine alone.

Made in the USA
San Bernardino, CA
14 March 2018